DREAMS

**Ten stories
of personal striving**

1st edition: March 2007
© Hospes Hotels & Moments
© Aldeas Infantiles SOS
© RBA Libros S.A.
Pérez Galdós, 36 – 08012 Barcelona
www.rbalibros.com

Coordination: Bonalletra, S.L.
Design and layout: Xavier Peralta
Photos: Mauricio Mergold

Ref. OAIS279
ISBN: 9788478719716
Legal deposit: B-13354-2007
Impression: Novagràfik (Barcelona)

DREAMS

**Ten stories
of personal striving**

RBA

HOSPES

Aldeas Infantiles SOS de España

Contents

Sleep and Dreams

Sueño. Does any word have greater or more elevated connotations? *Sueño*, understood as sleep, is a physiological necessity, something that is essential for us to be able to live our lives. But *sueño* understood as a dream is a longing, a desire, an aim – something that seems unattainable yet might be just around the corner if a little effort and willpower is applied. *Sueño*, then, is rest and relaxation, but it is also restlessness.

At Hospes we are aware of the enormous importance of both meanings of the word *sueño* in this complicated business that is life. For this reason, more than a year ago, we set up a social responsibility project named "Sueños", an ambitious project that aims to extol the best human and scientific values related to the two concepts of *sueño*.

The book you are reading summarises one of the two branches of the "Sueño" Project: *sueño* as a dream, an objective, a goal to strive for. Ten young people from Aldeas Infantiles SOS (SOS Children's Villages) are our protagonists, examples of strength, bravery and passionate striving to fulfil their personal and professional dreams in the face of the complex lives they have had to lead. The other branch of this exciting project, *sueño* as sleep, the source of health and well-being, is reflected in another book, "Sleeping, Dreaming and Resting: The Keys to Revitalising Sleep", an interesting exploration of these three ideas with recommendations that will help the reader to sleep deeply and awake refreshed.

Dreams, ten stories of striving to overcome personal difficulties

Everything begins with a dream. To be able to fly, to reach your goal, to create a family, to travel to the moon… It is in our hands to make these dreams come true. However, for the jostling images that throng together and make up our dream to become reality, to occupy a real physical space, to become tangible…, it is necessary to fight, to suffer and to bring out the best in ourselves.

During childhood it is our parents who teach us values such as the importance of loving what we do, or hard work as the infallible tool for turning our dreams into reality. They are there when our strength fails us or when we are overwhelmed by unexplained pessimism. Their simple presence helps us to overcome those difficult moments we all go through until the strength and energy that flow from optimism return.

There are children, now young people, who waited unavailingly to hear the voice of their parents, those beings that were everything for them, and who are still waiting. Hours, days, months, years went by. They struggled to find inside themselves the light that could once more illuminate their lives, searched for, and found, the energy to feed their dreams, big and small, and in the process made themselves bigger, stronger.

Sueños – Dreams brings together a series of stories in which the main characters are young people who have not resigned themselves to their complex situation, but rather have striven to overcome their difficulties. This book contains the stories and the images of these people who, despite losing their parents, their whole family, have continued to struggle to meet their objectives, to fulfil their dreams... The stories gathered here all share certain values like strength of will, self-discipline and optimism... all crowned by the same motto: "If you really want to, you can".

This second facet of *Sueños* is an antidote to superfluity, to hedonism as an attitude with which to face life. It confronts us with what we could do for ourselves, for our friends, for our work..., if only we were prepared to follow the path taken by these anonymous people who inspire us with what they have done.

To sum up, then, *Sueños* is an example of how social action inevitably generates respect and admiration for those people at whom it is directed. In exchange, Hospes receives energy, strength, commitment and will.

The "Sueños" Project is an important and necessary part of the Hospes model. It is a basic ingredient that allows us to create products and services of the highest value and benefit for society, so that people of whatever social class, religion or creed can sleep, dream and awake refreshed as a first step towards personal growth and improvement.

ANTONIO PÉREZ NAVARRO,
Managing Director of Hospes

ACKNOWLEDGEMENTS

I would like to place on record my gratitude to all those people involved in, and committed to this project, such as the **members of the *Sueños*** Jury, Eduard Estivill (President of the Jury), Juan Belda (Honorary President of the *Sueños* Jury and President of Aldeas Infantiles SOS), Francisco Javier Puertas (Secretary of the *Sueños* Jury and President of the AIPS – the Iberian Association of Sleep Pathology), Teresa Sagalés (AIPS), Ramón Rubio (AIPS), Francisco López (Aldeas Infantiles SOS), Marta Cardona (Aldeas Infantiles SOS), Fernando Morón (Aldeas Infantiles SOS), Almudena Cid (Olympic gymnast) and Rafael Beaus (member of the Board of FEIQUE); the **staff and Board Members of Hospes**, Mariano Fernández-Peña (President of Hospes), José Leoncio Areal, José Luis Blanco, Pedro Cortina, Antonio Hernández López, Alicia Koplowitz, Rafael López-Diéguez de Gamoneda, Juan Carlos Pradas, Mariano Yera Miranda, María Yera and Natalia Yera, the **author** of the book *Sueños* – Dreams, Joan Miquel Llodrà, the **photographer**, Mauricio Mergold, **other collaborators** who have participated directly in the project, like Cristina Serret, Cel·la Mondéjar, Dolors González, Maite Ciruela, Oriol Renart, Gina Rosell, Asis Casals and the team from SCPF, especially Ignasi Puig and Toni Segarra; to the whole **Hospes** team for their hard work, and to many other people who have supported us in this project and with whose help we will be able to make not only our own dreams come true – we can make the dreams of others come true too.

A book about hard work and striving to overcome difficulties

Amongst the best projects organised in collaboration with Aldeas Infantiles SOS de España (the Spanish branch of SOS Children's Villages) particularly outstanding is '*Sueños*', an initiative by Hospes, a company that offers support wherever it is needed. This attempt to reward the efforts of a group of young people who have made their own way in life, despite their difficult childhood, is worthy of a wider recognition. The awarding of scholarships to enable them to continue their studies is, for them, a magnificent stimulus.

This book, with its ten stories of the lives of hard-working young people, represents an eloquent testimony to those other young people who are struggling to make themselves independent.

It is essential that we are clear that what is needed is support for the development of the personality of the young people themselves and not its substitution by the personality of the educator. In these stories it seems evident that Aldeas Infantiles SOS takes care not to "smother" the young people, setting out rather to accompany them, providing them with the resources they need, not only financial but of every kind, with the aim of facilitating the development of their own values. It is they who have to make the effort; it is not a question of substituting this, but of promoting it.

It is important not to be in too much of a hurry with the process of becoming independent, but neither to remain passive bystanders: it is necessary to push a little, to reinforce the process. In short, it is necessary to maintain a balance between the two tendencies, something which is not always easy.

In some of the experiences described here, the young people talk about how they see their brothers and sisters, their companions, who have been in too much of a hurry to become independent before time, to earn their first wages. They have failed to develop fully, even though Aldeas Infantiles SOS still offers the resources they need to do so. Then they see their mistake, but it is too late.

For the professionals and the management of Aldeas Infantiles SOS, reading this book will, no doubt, be profoundly satisfying, not only for the acknowledgement of their work that the young people express in their accounts, though that itself is very encouraging, but also because it makes clear how the young people are making their own way in life, using the tools that have been made available to them and developing the values they have learnt.

This publication will be very useful for hundreds of young people and will motivate the 'SOS mothers', the educators, and the support workers to keep on working with the same level of enthusiasm and commitment.

Our gratitude to the "Sueños" Project is evident, especially to Antonio Pérez Navarro and Blanca Quintana Seguí, who have led this social commitment project from Hospes. Finally we would like to express our gratitude to Joan Miquel Llodrà, who has listened impartially to the experiences and the bravery of the young people he interviewed and has leavened them with observations of his own. If anybody from within Aldeas Infantiles SOS had written this book, it would have appeared as if they had an interest in exaggerating the work of the professionals in the organisation. He, however, coming from outside, is a more credible observer and commentator. He should also be congratulated for having captured, very faithfully, the language of the young people themselves.

JUAN BELDA,
President of Aldeas Infantiles SOS de España

Aldeas Infantiles SOS, helping children

Aldeas Infantiles SOS (SOS Children's Villages) is a private children's aid organisation, international, non-profit making, interconfessional and independent of any political orientation.

Our aim is to provide the children entrusted to us with a family setting, a stable home and a solid education so as to give them a promising and secure future. The organisation adopts a family model that is universal in character, but whose content is defined by the social and cultural realities of each country.

Around the world there are 457 SOS Children's Villages and 1268 SOS institutions, that is, Youth Houses, schools, hospitals, etc. The organisation operates in 132 countries, attending to the needs of approximately 300,000 children and young people, and is run by SOS Kinderdorf International (SOS International Children's Villages), which is the Federation of all the National Associations of SOS Children's Villages.

Aldeas Infantiles SOS has been present in Spain since 1967. In 1981, the Aldeas Infantiles SOS de España Association was set up to coordinate work at a national level and two years later it was declared an institution of 'public utility' by the Spanish Government's Council of Ministers. The Honorary President is H.R.H. the Prince of Asturias.

Aldeas Infantiles SOS de España runs eight Children's Villages: Barcelona, Pontevedra, Madrid, Granada, Cuenca, Santa Cruz de Tenerife, Zaragoza and Las Palmas and seven Villages in Latin America: Choluteca (Honduras), Lima (Peru), Mar del Plata (Argentina), Ricaurte and Portoviejo (Ecuador), Tijuana (Mexico) and San Jerónimo (Guatemala).

In Spain there is also a series of centres and programmes integrated into the Social Programme Centres, which complement the work of SOS Children's Villages and meet the growing social demands in the area of children and young people at risk: Day Centres; Nurseries; Outreach Youth Work Programmes; Advice Services to meet the needs of the young people who have passed through the organisation; Centres for Emergency Accommodation, Evaluation and Diagnosis; Family Educator Programmes; Special Employment Workshops, etc. In total, Aldeas Infantiles SOS de España looks after more than 3,400 children and young people.

In addition, it has a National Training School in Granada to enable all its staff to update their knowledge by attending courses and day-conferences that deal with issues connected with children.

Should you require further information about the work
of Aldeas Infantiles SOS visit our website at
www.aldeasinfantiles.es
or phone
(34) 902 33 22 22

Contact:
Gracia Escudero, directora de Comunicación
Aldeas Infantiles SOS de España
Tel: (34) 91 388 45 49
Fax: (34) 91 388 67 47

THE DELIBERATIONS OF THE JURY

"How can we choose just three?"

Ten candidates, three study grants and a project aimed at making the dreams of three young people from Aldeas Infantiles SOS come true. The members of the Jury, who had to decide who to award the prizes to, felt weighed down by the responsibility. In their hands they had ten stories and, for them, all were worthy winners.

They were gathered in a room in the Hospes Amérigo hotel in Alicante, and just one hour later they would have to announce the winners of the awards. Some days earlier, each of them had received a dossier with the stories of the ten candidates. Young men and women from several different Aldeas in Spain who had managed to overcome enormous difficulties and set about acquiring an education had set out, in short, on a life of their own. The first question they had to discuss was, then, what criteria to use in choosing the winners. In the eyes of the Jury all of them were worthy of being chosen. Should they reward the best academic results? Since study grants were being offered, this would seem to be reasonable. But the aim of these awards was to recognise those who could serve as an example to others, a model of struggling against and eventually overcoming difficulties. How could they rule out anybody, for in every case, what they had achieved represented an enormous personal triumph?

One member of the Jury summed up the dilemma perfectly: "We were not evaluating scientific works, we were evaluating lives, and that made us feel responsible for the future of the young people".

The members of the Jury began their deliberations. One by one they went over the stories of the young people and soon came to realise how difficult it was going to be to take a decision.

They all agreed not to simply reward a brilliant academic career, nor did they want to transmit the idea that only by being successful in educational terms could you be a winner. However, they could not ignore the fact that academic achievements also involved a great deal of hard work and a spirit of self-sacrifice.

Thus, they decided to reward academic careers. But then, on top of that, some further clarification was needed... At this point, one of the members of the Jury came up with a synthesis in the form of a triangle of what, for him, should be the result of the deliberations. Each side would represent a virtue, as personified by one of the young people. On one side they had already decided to place educational success. On the second would be the idea of dedication, the capacity to give of themselves to the benefit of others, to act out of generosity while, at the same time, developing their own personal life project. Finally, on the third side, they would seek to reward ongoing effort, constant hard work despite the limitations under which the young person was labouring.

The deliberations had come to an end and the function room of the hotel was packed to overflowing. Soon the names of the prize winners would be announced. Three names, three scholarships, and under the watchful gaze of all those present, the ten candidates, all of them winners.

Dreams 2005 Jury was formed by:

DR. EDUARD ESTIVILL,
President of the Jury. Paediatrician and Clinical Neurophysiologist.

DRA. TERESA SAGALÉS,
AIPS – Iberian Association of Sleep Pathology.

DR. RAMÓN RUBIO,
AIPS – Iberian Association of Sleep Pathology.

ANTONIO PÉREZ NAVARRO,
Managing Director of Hospes.

FRANCISCO LÓPEZ,
Director of the Training School of Aldeas Infantiles SOS.

MARTA CARDONA,
Director of the Training School of Aldeas Infantiles SOS.

FERNANDO MORÓN,
Aldeas Infantiles SOS – Corporate Relations.

ALMUDENA CID,
Olympic gymnast.

RAFAEL BEAUS,
Pharmacist, Member of the Board of FEIQUE.

BREOGÁN: FROM GALICIAN
MYTH TO PRESENT DAY HERO

Breogán, the mythological father of the Galician people, credited, amongst other feats, with the building of what is known today as the 'Torre de Hércules', in A Coruña, is also the name of our young hero, Breogán Sobral. The life of our Breogán, born twenty-four years ago in the Galician town of Sanxenxo, with all its heroic deeds and misfortunes, is comparable in many senses to that of any classical hero. A life made up of both good and bad moments which, sooner or later is rewarded for everything that has been attained through hard work and tenacity. The mythological Breogán is remembered in the Galician national anthem; the real one, the one sitting in front of me, is, I am sure, remembered by all those who have played a part in his life.

We meet in the offices of the Galician Aldeas Infantiles SOS in Vigo. There he has been waiting for me, since early morning, together with David Lago, a companion of his for some years in Aldeas. I suppose it is a fairly typical day in this area: cool, cloudy and with a persistent drizzle that never quite manages to become rain. Elvira, a worker with Aldeas, attentive to our needs at all times, serves us coffee and biscuits. Very welcome.

Breogán seems a little ill at ease at first. He doesn't know why I am there, sitting in front of him, prepared with my tape recorder to capture every word he utters. But he is not too mistrustful and after chatting for a few moments, during which I explained what I was after, he begins to describe in general terms the main events of his life. Little by little, he starts to open up, describing things in detail. I give him absolute freedom – he is the hero of this tale.

A difficult childhood

The story of Breogán is like that of many other young people who have found themselves forced to cope without the support that comes from a certain degree of family and financial stability. From when he was very young, Breogán has had to face numerous obstacles and difficulties of various kinds that, fortunately, he has managed to overcome. His family's problems have undoubtedly left their mark on him; indeed, as he is willing to admit, they continue to affect him, though as the years have gone by he has learnt to deal with that.

I am surprised by the frankness with which Breogán begins to explain some aspects of his life, things which others might try to cover up. He is very sincere with me, at that time a stranger to him, something I find admirable.

When he was only five years old, Breogán was taken into a residential institution for the first time. His parents' financial and health problems forced them to take the decision. But after four months of incessant tears, his grandmother took him out of the centre. Unfortunately, her death two years later, and the fact that his grandfather found it impossible to look after Breogán and his brother, meant that the two boys went back into care, this time for good. Thus, from the age of seven to thirteen Breogán lived in various institutions. This was a time of constant moves, something that he describes as if it were very normal, just one more part of his life, an odyssey that took him to the towns of Sanxenxo, Pontevedra, Seixo, Bueu and Abrente.

Though at the beginning life in these institutions was very hard for him and he was very unhappy, he managed to get used to it. There, surrounded by other boys in similar situations, the worst thing, he says, is not the discrimination you face from others, but your own, the self-discrimination, as he puts it. At this point in the conversation, Breogán does not let himself get carried away by his emotions, instead simply presenting facts, memories and experiences with an absolute serenity, with no nostalgia, but also with no reproaches.

Coming into contact with Aldeas Infantiles SOS

At the age of thirteen, in the middle of his adolescence, Breogán left the home to live for a time with his father – his parents are separated, he adds. But things went wrong again when his father's illness reappeared. This led the young Breogán to fail the year at school and he returned to the children's home. Once he had completed the third year of 'BUP' (secondary school education, roughly equivalent to British GCSEs), Breogán's path crossed with that of Aldeas Infantiles SOS, El Jardín de las Hespérides, the house in which, at the age of sixteen, he was to find the warmth of a family home. For Aldeas, from 1999 onwards, was to change his life, and for this, he will always be profoundly grateful to them.

In the Aldeas Infantiles SOS Youth House in Vigo, Breogán was to discover an atmosphere that was completely different from that of the institutions he had known until that time. The educators showed him how to be more grown up, to take on responsibilities, simply how to live for himself. He had to take control of his own life, from something as basic as getting himself up on time, to dealing with the forms he had to fill in during his contact with the authorities, something that Breogán had never had to worry about up until then.

He recalls, in an amusing way, the first payment he received and that he had to learn how to administer; he couldn't believe it, it was the first time in his life that something like this had happened to him. They called him to the Director's office. He thought he was going to be told off for doing something wrong but, to his surprise, they handed him an envelope with money inside. Incredible! In the retelling of this episode, Breogán displays a fine sense of irony verging, at times, on sarcasm, a sense of humour that I was to discover is very much part of his character.

Life in Aldeas Infantiles SOS turned out to be an initiation rite into the adult world, one that aimed to cultivate Breogán's independence and autonomy. Aldeas has had a very strong influence on all aspects of his short life, but especially on his emotional education. He defines himself as a 'hard person', but all heroes, no matter how hard they might seem, have a heart inside them that ends up revealing itself. It was to be later that this heart showed itself more fully, when speaking of his family and his relationship with them.

Breogán has always done well at school though sometimes, as he is willing to recognise, he has not done as much as he could have. When he was small, he didn't have to try very hard – without making any great effort he passed all his subjects. 'EGB' (basic, general education, normally from 7 to 14 years of age) went well, as did BUP, despite having to repeat the second year. He is fully aware that the little work he did was more than enough for him to pass the exams with ease.

The bad memories of that time are related to the moments of conflict with his family, with his parents or with his elder brother. On occasions, circumstances led him to give the appearance of being a bad student; his attendance in class was irregular and he spent many hours out on the streets, in order to be at home as little as possible. He tells me he felt lost, and that on occasions he felt like grabbing his things, stuffing them into his bag and running away. However, his maturity showed through – he realised that he was only a child and he wouldn't get very far. Fortunately, Breogán overcame the difficulties and managed to clamber out of the hole he found himself in. Shortly afterwards, he entered the Aldeas Infantiles SOS family, a fact that kept him from going off the rails.

On completing 'COU' (Sixth Form studies, roughly equivalent to British A levels), Breogán decided to follow a difficult path. Unlike other young people in Aldeas who, at a particular age, decide to start work, he opted to continue with his studies – this is the challenge he set himself. At no time did he consider being a builder like his father, and he says this not as a form of recrimination. Simply, as his tone of voice shows, he began to be very clear about what he wants and what he doesn't want from life.

A new adventure to live

Thus began our hero's new adventure: entering the Physics Faculty at the University of Santiago de Compostela, a city in which, in his view, there is much more of a student life than in Vigo. He chose this course without giving any thought to the possible work opportunities he would find on graduating; he likes mathematics, sciences and physics; he finds them easy and for him this was more then enough of a reason. In addition, the idea of being in Santiago, where he first lived in a student hall of residence and where he is now sharing a flat with friends and other students, is another of the attractions that led him to register in the Physics Faculty.

The first year at university was quite hard. The high school years in which, with just a little work, he could pass without any great difficulty were now a thing of the past. His poor academic results during the first year were, however, compensated for by the number of new people he met and the friendships he struck up.

Breogán, who is very clear about his objective, does not give up easily and in the second year, by dint of some very serious studying and a little more discipline, he managed to make good all he had lost or fallen behind with in the first year. His success in passing Mechanics 2, with which he had struggled mightily, filled him with pride and, no doubt, the enthusiasm he needed to continue. Even today, when he remembers it, he can't help giving a sigh of relief. Perhaps the thing he liked least about his time at university was the excessively academic atmosphere, especially where the lecturers were concerned. He remains a little disappointed about this, feeling that many of his teachers did not display a human quality on a par with their enormous academic knowledge.

Having completed his five years at university, Breogán moved on to specialise in Radiophysics – working with gamma rays, x-rays… He explains that his original intention was to stay on in the faculty, working on a doctoral programme or collaborating in some other way, but with time he came to realise that he didn't like the atmosphere and that he wouldn't be happy working there. Listening to him, it's clear that the idea of so many people being cooped up in the same room, surrounded by computers, doesn't hold many attractions for him.

To be able to study Radiophysics, Breogán had to overcome a new obstacle: a pretty stiff exam but one that, if he passed, would enable him to do three years of practical work and thus qualify as a radiophysicist. Breogán knew that during these three years he might well have to move to some other part of Spain, far from his native Galicia. But this did not deter him, quite the contrary. He also confessed to me, half joking, half serious, that one of his plans for the future involves living in a city that has a First Division football team so he can go and watch matches at the weekend. Not much does he ask from life…

Despite having come of age, Aldeas Infantiles SOS continues to finance Breogán's studies, though he also receives some money from the government in the form of a grant and has savings from the various temporary jobs he's done. In this way his future as a student is guaranteed for the moment, until such time as he is able to support himself.

Breogán has been conscious, ever since he first entered Aldeas Infantiles SOS, that a good academic education is an essential condition for finding a good job, whether in Spain or abroad. In terms of his professional career, it has to be said that his ambitions are fairly limited – he simply wants a quiet life without too many headaches. Laughing, he says he doesn't want to work too hard. This might sound bad, but he explains further and clarifies what he means. Money is not his main aim in life, and neither does he want to be a slave to his work. It is clear that the ice has been well and truly broken now and Breogán feels free to explain himself fully, at least in some things…

He hopes that when he finds a good job as a radiophysicist, he will be able to combine the eight hours of the working day, plus any on-call shifts he might have to do, with his favourite pastimes: *el terraceo* – watching people go by while savouring a good beer, doing sports, like basketball, football or any other team game, and especially his electric guitar, an instrument that he has taught himself to play since the age of thirteen and that has led him to become a regular visitor to some of the music bars and clubs in Santiago. His guitar has also helped him, on more than one occasion, to escape from the world around him. Though he considers himself to be a very realistic person, with his feet firmly on the ground, from time to time he needs to escape into his own world. One of the many dreams floating through Breogán's mind is that of being able to dedicate himself at some point to music, to play in a jazz band, far removed from commercial mass-produced music.

But all that is in the future. Today, Breogán explains that he is satisfied; he could be better, he says, somewhat resignedly, but he has no complaints. He feels proud of himself, of all that he has achieved thanks, in part, to his fighting spirit. He is also proud of his capacity to better himself, to constantly improve, and of the positive attitude he tries to maintain at all times. However, he recognises that he has never considered being at the top or at the bottom; he has always simply allowed himself to go with the flow. The challenges, he says, you set yourself for the long term, and with time, you find yourself moving, more or less, along your path. When I think about how old he is, I realise how mature he is when it comes to discussing certain things.

Portrait of a modern hero

In general he considers himself to be an optimist – and having spoken with him I can confirm this, a person who tries to face up to life in a positive way. Negative thoughts, obviously, he also has, particularly when he feels alone. Like everybody who ever walked this planet, Breogán from time to time feels down, especially when he has to deal with the health problems that also affect his mother and elder brother – he hasn't seen his father for some years now. These are things that have marked his life and that, in fact, continue to worry him.

I ask him if, as a child, he envied his friends with a more conventional family life, without any apparent financial or emotional difficulties. He admits that, from time to time, he had felt jealous of them. Though sometimes it is unavoidable, he doesn't like feeling like this and he has learnt not to allow himself to do so, reckoning that it leads nowhere. For many years now Breogán has been aware that his family has problems and that he has to learn to live with this. Sometimes this situation annoys him, he freely admits, but it is necessary to accept it. However, on some occasions, if he sees that he can do nothing about a particular problem, he chooses to run away from it. At the same time, he tends not to explain his doubts or problems to his family so as not to worry them more – they already have enough on their plate, he says, which means he often has to pretend that everything is fine. From what he tells me, he has learnt to put his feelings to one side when necessary. I sense that in this part of his life Breogán has contradictory feelings, though he seems to cope with this quite well.

Breogán does not see himself as being different from other people; he knows that everybody has problems, more or less serious. But faced with this he has managed to develop his own system of defence. Not for him laser beams, or the waves of his hero Songoku, no, he simply uses laughter. Breogán loves joking and laughing; as he says, they are his greatest protection against adversity, and doubtless the best way of making friends. Though he says he is a home-loving person, he also likes going out till all hours, like any other young man of his age. Going out, being surrounded by other people, allows him to relax and not think too much. I realise this when, once the interview was over, we all go out into Vigo to go and have a drink. Breogán, David Lago, the photographer and me. It is then that Breogán displays his full sense of humour, sometimes very direct, sometimes highly subtle.

Breogán is aware of his strong points, but also of his weaknesses; his virtues and his defects. In some ways he might seem to lack discipline or be prone to run away from moments of conflict when perhaps he should stand his ground; but nobody is perfect, not superheroes, and certainly not twenty-four-year-old lads. Despite everything, what most stands out about him is that both his family and his friends can always count on him. He knows that, by talking to them, he has the capacity to relax and reassure those who come to him looking for support or advice; there are even some people who, as a result, call him the 'valium boy': the image is powerful.

His family, who he frequently visits, and friends are very important for Breogán and he tries to look after them as much as he can. Not in the least selfish, he sees that the ability to live with others is crucially important in all areas of life, both emotional and professional. The lack of companionship is something he detests in the society of today, especially at work. He has no doubt that learning to live alongside others, and with himself, is one of the most important things that Breogán has got from his time with Aldeas Infantiles SOS.

Breogán is interested, and worried, by politics, the situation of the world in general, and he is indignant about the individualism that dominates society, the false idea of progress being pushed everywhere, consumerism, corruption or unbridled ambition. Breogán is a lad with values and principles, the result of his very intense experiences of life. If one day he has children, he intends to bring them up with these ideas, though he will try to allow them to lead the life they choose. He would like to give them enough freedom to choose their own path, though he knows this is difficult given the tendency to over-protect which seems inherent in the condition of being a parent.

Our particular hero is, despite everything, a lad of his time, and one who worries about the times in which he lives. What Breogán is very clear about is that the American dream does not exist; the only dreams that exist are those we all carry within us and that, with work and strength of will, might just come true. I think he's absolutely right…

The faces
of the
dreamers

Ten young people who have
spent part of their lives in
Aldeas Infantiles SOS share
their experiences and hopes
for the future with us.

Breogán, student of Physics, specialising in Radiophysics.
His interests include the electric guitar, ballgames and he would like to live in a city that has a First Division football team. Below, Breogán with his friend David.

Breogán arrived in the Youth House 'El jardín de las Hespérides' at the age of sixteen, having spent time in various residential institutions. Health and financial problems in his family led him to Aldeas Infantiles SOS. According to Breogán, there he learnt to be a complete person.

David entered the Aldeas Infantiles SOS home at the age of thirteen. There he discovered the pleasure of studying 'with' books. He says that he also learnt to listen to his heart as well as to his mind.

David is working on his graduation project, which will enable him to become a fully-fledged Mining Engineer, specialising in energy.

He would like to spend some time working abroad, but he's not very confident of being able to convince his mother that going away would be good for him.

Lorena, seen here with Esperanza and Juan Carlos, arrived in Aldeas Infantiles SOS at the age of twelve, together with her seven brothers and sisters. She has studied to be an Infant Teacher though she has realised what she really likes is working in a Primary School. She'll have to find some solution to this...

Lorena, on the left, is studying to be an Infant School Teacher in the University of Segovia.

Esperanza, below, is doing a Higher Level course in Audiovisuals specialising in Television Production.

Juan Carlos is studying in the Faculty
of Architecture in Madrid.
*De pequeño quería ser policía aunque ahora
sus héroes son los arquitectos famosos.*

Esperanza, here seen with Lorena and Juan
Carlos, arrived in Aldeas in September 1998
to undergo an operation to correct lateral
spinal curvature. Apart from working hard
at her studies and other chores, she is
undergoing a rehabilitation programme that
involves physiotherapy and swimming.

At the age of ten, Juan Carlos was taken into the Aldea in Cuenca, together with his two brothers. He is very clear that when he finishes he has no intention of continuing his studies…, though a Master's might always come in handy.

Mamen arrived in Aldeas Infantiles SOS in Granada, with her four brothers and sisters, when she was three. She is considering registering for INEF to be doubly qualified and thus better positioned when it comes to getting a permanent teaching job.

Inma, on the left, is studying for Mid-Level qualification in Business Administration and Management. *She admits she doesn't much like studying but sees it's necessary to get ahead.*

Mamen, is doing Teacher Training, specialising in Physical Education. *She defines herself as a radical when it comes to talking about the role of women in the society of today. Her friends say that she takes after her educator in Aldeas in this.*

Inma entered Aldeas Infantiles SOS when she was five, with her brothers and sisters. She would like to find a job as an administration assistant in a financial consultancy, an estate agent's or a building company, but it has to be in Granada!

43

Rubí, on the left, is studying a module in Administration and Finance.

When she was small what she liked best was to gaze at the stars and the planets through her telescope.

Rubí and her two brothers arrived in Aldeas when she was thirteen. She will soon return to her studies in Business Administration and Management in the Faculty of Economics and Business Studies at the University of Granada.

Jonathan arrived in Aldeas at the age of seventeen, together with his younger brothers. His secret is to set himself small, short-term goals and try to achieve them steadily. When it comes to dreaming, he would like to manage a company.

Jonathan, on the left, has just finished his Higher Level course in Administration.
He enjoyed the two-month placement he did in the University Hospital and would love to find a job there.

Sonia is studying Graphic Design and she would like to work in publishing design.
Thanks to the advice of a trainer, she is now able to combine her studies with playing tennis and at the same time make some money.

Sonia was taken into Aldeas as a baby, when she was just a few months old. She explains that the proof that she has grown up is that she is now training young children and, what is sometimes more difficult, dealing successfully with their parents. She would like to spend some time in an English-speaking city, as she has already done in Chicago.

DAVID: THE STORY
OF A ONCE-SHY YOUNG MAN

Behind this shy, retiring boy hides a young man who is proud of the fact that he has made himself what he is. His story, like that of many other young people, is one of overcoming personal difficulties.

Our meeting takes place in Vigo, to be exact, in the offices that Aldeas Infantiles SOS has in this Galician town. I arrive there having come straight from the airport; Elvira leads me to the room where David is waiting for me, accompanied by Breogán Sobral. After talking to the latter, I begin my conversation with David. His physical size and seriousness are a little off-putting at first. I think that it's going to be a difficult job, but I soon realise that I'm wrong about that. After making my brief presentation, David begins to participate freely in the conversation.

Yesterday

In 1994, at the age of fourteen, due to family problems David was taken into the Aldea in Redondela (Pontevedra). Till then he had never lived in a residential centre, and he defines this episode as a turning point in his life. He himself describes this organisation

49

as offering the best solution to his personal situation, an enormous change compared with what he had lived up until that time – the conviction with which he states this is more than sufficient confirmation. Two years later, David moved to the Aldeas Infantiles SOS Youth House in Vigo, where he spent the first year of his university course.

The small number of people David lived with in both homes, his companions and the staff charged with looking after them, meant that he soon struck up strong relationships based on friendship and affection with them. In Aldeas Infantiles SOS David found a series of strangers who soon became his family. There they gave him what had been lacking at home, his parents being separated, and the family's stability being undermined by their financial difficulties.

David was born and spent his childhood in a rural setting, in the Galician village of Porriño. He explains that farm work helped to compensate the family's meagre income. His father's absence meant that from a very young age he had to take on the role of being responsible for the home. Conscious of the family's situation, he soon realised that he, as the elder brother, had to look after his small family – his mother and sister.

David does not remember much of his adolescence, and in truth it's quite understandable. Had he been in a position to choose, he would have preferred a different life; a little more 'liberal', as he puts it. Going out at night, having fun with friends or simply enjoying life without having to think about problems were things David simply could not afford to do – he had obligations to meet. Now he wonders what his life would have been like if he had been a teenager like other boys of his age. What would have become of him? It seems to me, from the way in which he frames this question, that he is not particularly interested in the answer. The present is what counts.

From when he was small, David was interested in studying, despite the various difficulties he faced. School was a good three kilometres from his house, and so, every day, rain or shine, warm or cold, he was faced with a long walk through the woods before he could even sit behind his desk. His future seemed to be that of the majority of other local boys: finish school and find a job in whatever was going. David could have opted for building work or other manual trades, but he wanted more from life, he saw that he was good at school and so decided to start his sixth-form studies. It is clear that the young man had caught a glimpse of what was to be his path through life.

David liked going to the library. Introverted and shy as he was – and continues to be – this turned out to be the ideal space in which to take refuge from all that surrounded him while also allowing him to continue learning. He has many memories of that time; some were, I suppose, not very funny at the time but they make him smile now. David is beginning to look more relaxed. During his first year of BUP, for example, he applied for a grant that, as a result of various instances of negligence beyond his control, was never awarded to him. He found himself, then, with only one textbook, since his family's resources would not stretch to more. Thus, he spent the whole year copying, taking notes and asking his friends for help. To all this should be added the fact that nobody in his family had ever managed to finish EGB, and so the time arrived when the only person who could help him solve the problems he had with his homework was David himself, and then only with a great deal of effort. Despite this he managed to keep going, passing his school years with fives, sixes and the occasional seven.

All this was to change when David arrived at Aldeas Infantiles SOS: "Having all the books you need is fantastic!" he exclaims. The years went by and he managed to complete his science-based COU. He was quite good at arts subjects but he found them boring, just studying and memorising, according to him – I disagree, but that is another story. Sciences, on the other hand, offered him much more. He explains that this was a decisive moment in his life, a moment to look for ways out, to find new paths. He thought about joining the Army, a good place to be trained, earn a salary, and after some years, graduate. However, his family, seeing that this would mean his leaving, opposed the idea. In terms of studying at university, David first considered doing Aeronautics in Madrid, but once more the argument was the same: his family thought that the capital was too far away for him to be studying there. That was when he opted for Mining Engineering, the main attractions being that there was very little unemployment among graduates and the fact that he could study in his native Galicia.

Today

The important thing is that what is past is past, though David, aware of just how heavily it weighs, never loses sight of it – he doesn't need to say so for you to realise this. This young man from Galicia is about to become a mining engineer. If anybody had told him this ten years ago, he would never have believed it.

David has thus become the first person in his family to study at university and, it hardly needs saying, his mother, like almost all mothers, cannot help talking proudly about her son and his diplomas. Looking back, David realises that he has met almost all the objectives he has set himself in his life. The journey, however, has not been easy.

When he chose to leave the Aldeas Infantiles SOS Youth House, by then a student at university, David went to live in one of the Halls of Residence, since he understood that this was the best place to be if he wanted to do well at university. Later, he decided to live alone, outside Vigo, the city in which he studies. At present, Aldeas Infantiles SOS continues to meet part of the cost of this flat, which is in Pontearas. David administers the money he receives, spending it on his needs and duly justifying any movements to those in charge at Aldeas. He himself is responsible for using the money in whatever way he chooses as long as he can vouch for it.

David likes living alone, though he recognises it is not ideal; for him, doing the housework is much worse than trying to resolve a mathematical equation. Almost everything he knows about these domestic chores he learnt during the years he spent in Aldeas Infantiles SOS when, despite there being workers who looked after them, they had to learn to take care of themselves in terms of managing their own accommodation. He confesses that on more than one occasion he has thought of trying to invent a machine that would do in a flash all the household chores that he finds so difficult. He imagines a device that would trap all the dust and all he would have to do is press a button, but then he supposes it must already have been invented…

David, despite living independently, continues to stay in close contact with his family, who he has always had a good relationship with. He considers himself to be a stabilising force, helping to maintain the tranquillity and balance within the family. His mother and sister see him as their most solid support, the pillar that helps to compensate for the ups and downs that appear from time to time – he says all this with a conviction that seems studied and almost off pat. According to him, if the family is okay, he is okay. David, as far as he is able to, helps them financially, getting them through their financial rough patches and frequently giving them money. He considers it to be his obligation, though his family have always encouraged him to go on studying.

David describes himself as a supportive person, helping when and how he can, not only his family but also the people around him, both friends and neighbours. As he puts it, it's necessary to look out for others, you can't turn your back on the world, and so he actively participates in anything that might prove useful for others. In the meetings of the neighbours who share his stairwell, for example, he tries to do his bit helping in whatever way he can, with all the knowledge he has; advising on the choice of the best aerial, sorting out the accounts or reminding them about the maintenance of the lift. His words might sound a little smug, but his tone of voice expresses humility.

David confesses that he owes much of what he is today to Aldeas Infantiles SOS and the workers there. He recognises that it was Aldeas that helped him to make something of himself. There he also put aside some of his shyness, though it continues to exist below the surface; instead, he has become more open, more extrovert, not so closed in on himself. At Aldeas, he says, they made him more of a person. Before, he was more rational, more methodical, colder – it was easier for him to confront his reality in that way, things were black or white, no time was wasted on contemplating shades of grey. Now, thanks to Aldeas, nuances exist for David. This change can be explained by the fact that he met people whose situations and histories were different from his own. This made him see things from another perspective. He knows exactly what he is talking about...

David, though it's difficult for him to admit it, feels proud of himself, of what he has achieved, and much more so bearing in mind his humble rural origins. Though he knows that there are much more significant things in life, money is fairly important for him, and he has no difficulty saying so, though often it is not correct to say so publicly. As he has learnt, money is the key to many of the things he was deprived of during his childhood and adolescence – a good education, for example. David greatly values all the material goods he possesses, not out of selfishness, but for the effort it took him to acquire them.

Though he knows that everything he has, and where he has got to, he has worked for himself, David is conscious that he has been very lucky. Apart from the circumstances, there is also his non-conformist attitude, his desire to better himself and his efforts to meet the targets he has set for himself. In addition, as he himself recognises, without the appearance of Aldeas Infantiles SOS, given the lack of resources in his family home, his life would probably have been very different.

Despite everything he has achieved to date, only the beginning I am sure, David never loses his head. He is interested in the state of the society we live in. He reads the newspapers every day and this helps him to keep up-to-date, informed about what is going on in the world, about politics, and the economy. Being well-informed is undoubtedly the best weapon, especially in the discussions he has almost every day with his friends from university and in which they talk about all kinds of questions affecting both the country and the planet as a whole. His opinions about a particular question are not fixed, it is a wise man who recognises the error of his ways, and David, if he is convinced by an argument, will happily change his mind.

The precariousness of the labour market, poverty or immigration are all things that preoccupy him and about which he has his own ideas. He is affected, for example, by the fact that Spain does not value its own workers, does not support researchers, and that these are often obliged to look for work elsewhere. Though he hopes that, sooner or later, the situation will change, David thinks that things are not very hopeful for his generation. He sees those around him as very committed and much more prepared than before, but also immersed in problems that did not exist before: the cost of buying a home, debts, unemployment... Problems that he is bound to face when he finishes university. Aware of the world we live in, David comments that either you join in or you are left out. The maturity of his point of view on many of the questions facing us surprises me. The conversation stretches out when we are talking of these things, but we must continue with his story.

Tomorrow

David, after five long and intense years of studying, is about to graduate as a Mining Engineer, specialising in energy. So many hours spent poring over books, at home or in the library, have been worth it. Now, he only has to finish his final project, and then he will be able to sign commissions as a fully-fledged engineer. Speaking of this project his eyes light up. And he already has many more projects in mind, most of them related to alternative energies. He explains, passionately, the possible production of hydrogen, a non-polluting source of energy, using the enormous potential for wind-power that Galicia has, largely wasted at present. He speaks to me, half serious, half joking, of the enormous quantity of methane generated by the flatulence of the thousands of cows grazing the meadows of Galicia, a gas that could also be used…

Once his project has been completed, David aspires, rather than to a very high salary, to becoming, above all, a good engineer. He hopes that when he is working he will be faced by challenges; it is not difficult to realise that this young man is not particularly attracted by the easy life, he needs to be continually stretched, to squeeze out of his mind the solutions to problems that might appear, to demonstrate fairly and squarely the whole of his potential. David, nevertheless, is not looking to get to the top; getting to the top of the heap is not what drives him, he says.

One of his objectives in the immediate future, once he has finished university, would be to go abroad, despite the fact that his family are not very enthusiastic about the idea. David is very clear about this; he could stay in Galicia, for example, and work in the granite quarries, but this idea does not attract him. He would like to work, if possible, for a multi-national company based in Algeria, one of the countries of South America or in China. In fact, if he doesn't go abroad, things look complicated to him, since Spain does not offer as many job opportunities in this area. In many parts of the world there are opportunities in the mining engineering field. Apart from making his living and travelling, an ambition he has had since he was very young, he could also satisfy his desire to see other cultures and get to know different people. The only obstacle he sees to all this, apart from having to convince his mother, is perhaps the question of languages, though he's had to deal with bigger problems than this before…

In terms of his emotional life, David is cautious, even reserved. He is very bold in all those things that have to do with his studies and the world of work, but in matters of the heart he feels a little ill at ease – for it is here, in the field of the emotions of another person, that one cannot be so rational or scientific. He is very aware of this and recognises that he would like to be more impulsive and to act more spontaneously, but that it is difficult for him. The emotions are one area of his life that, for now, he intends to leave to one side; perhaps, as he confesses to me, because of the bad experiences of relationships he has lived and seen at first hand – too many disappointments, he half whispers. We leave this question to one side...

David does not know if he will ever form a family of his own. He cannot imagine himself marrying in the next ten years. He says that with matters of the heart, it's difficult to predict. The idea of having children he sees as quite difficult, especially in terms of their education. David, in a tone that seems to me more sceptical than pessimistic, is aware that, the way things are going, bringing a child into the world is a very big responsibility. If, at some time in the future, he does become a father, he will try to inculcate in his children the values he has learnt over the years, particularly, the value of working hard, and of work well-done. If they want something, they should struggle for it, and if it is by studying, then so much the better. He is implacable on this.

I leave him, returning to the airport, with the impression that a brilliant future awaits him. I am sure I am not mistaken...

LORENA: A DEEPLY FELT FEELING

There are some who say that the maternal instinct is not biological but rather something that is socially or culturally determined. Different branches of science argue about this. When we talk about maternal instinct, or so I believe, we should not only understand the desire to be a mother, that is, to bring new life into the world, but also the need to care for and educate children, something that may spring simply from a strong sense of responsibility.

Some people are born with this maternal instinct while in others, with time and for various reasons, it develops later. There are some who never experience this feeling, yet this is not the case of our protagonist, Lorena. Her life, and the experiences she has lived through in her family, have led her to think of herself as more than just an elder sister, have led her to act as mother to her brothers and sisters. This also explains why she has decided to continue her studies in order to become a teacher.

We meet in Madrid, in the offices of Aldeas Infantiles SOS, near Avenida Arturo Soria. She is accompanied by Esperanza and Juan Carlos, colleagues of hers from Aldeas. The first thing I notice about her is her open healthy laughter, quite contagious. From the very outset Lorena shows herself to be jovial and extrovert, though at certain moments a shadow of seriousness seems to pass over her. Little by little, she will surprise me...

Growing up too quickly

Lorena Alarcón Ruiz was born twenty-three years ago in the Castilian town of Cuenca, part of a large family of eight children – she is the second. The financial situation of the family was not very good, a fact that led, after some years, to the separation of parents and children.

Lorena went to school like any other girl of her age, but her attendance record was very poor. While her mother was working, she and her sister Vanesa had to look after the rest of the children; her parents would have liked things to be different, but the situation they were in made it impossible. The truth is that, at that time, Lorena didn't care very much whether she went to school or not, for her principal obligations lay elsewhere. Who thinks about the future or the times to come when you are that age? Whenever she could, she went to school and she enjoyed it, just like the rest of the pupils of her age.

Though it may seem unlikely, Lorena has very fond memories of her somewhat haphazard schooling in Cuenca. There she went to a really great school, the same one that, years before, her mother and her uncles and aunts had attended. She remembers especially the time when the teacher said that if she didn't behave he would pull her pigtails just as he had done, years earlier, to her mother.

A change of life

She was taken into the Aldea de San Lorenzo de El Escorial, accompanied by her seven brothers and sisters, on 15 July 1995.

They were between three and fifteen years old. Fortunately, and as normally happens in Aldeas Infantiles SOS, they were not separated, and so they all ended up living in the same house, being looked after by the same educator.

The change in her life, as Lorena remembers it, was a little brusque because they went from living happily at home as a family, to living in an unknown place, amongst strangers and with children whose family history was very different from theirs. Children who, in the village, had a bad name, she explains. In addition, she couldn't understand why they had been moved to San Lorenzo de El Escorial when there was an Aldea in her native Cuenca. At that time, they didn't understand that physical distance from where they had been born and brought up was beneficial for them, to get them away a little from the situation they had lived up until then – not to get them away from their family, it must be understood. It was also explained to them that their situation was going to be temporary – it would only be for three or four months, until the financial situation of their parents, now separated, improved or at least stabilised. This improvement never came about, and so ever since then Lorena has stayed with Aldeas.

It was difficult at first to adapt to the new norms and rules, though it didn't take long for them to get used to their new life. The most important thing, she insists, was that they could all be together. Once in Aldeas, Lorena and Vanesa played the role of elder sisters or... of mothers! She believes that if they had been offered the chance to leave, they would have preferred to stay, because they lived much better there. They were fully aware of how well-off they were in Aldeas and that they couldn't afford to squander the opportunity they had been given. In fact, both she and her elder sister were offered the chance to stay in Cuenca, but in the end they decided that they would rather go to Madrid with their brothers and sisters. Sometimes the two of them wonder what would have become of them if they had stayed in Cuenca. They would surely have had to leave school and start work, each one looking out for herself... but in truth nobody knows the answer, and now it doesn't seem very important.

Even so, from time to time there were difficult moments – they missed the life in their home town. And in fact Lorena and her brothers and sisters were not able to go back to Cuenca until a year and a half after they were taken in. Meanwhile it was their mother who came to visit them, and they were able to talk to their grandparents and uncles and aunts by phone. Later on, there was no problem about seeing their relatives as often as they wished.

Lorena has met many educators, and with some of them she built up relations based on true affection. She tells me, thinking I suppose about the course she is doing, that she knows that this job can be a very hard one. The hours are long, she says, and there is a lot of responsibility. However, she also knows that there are educators who consider their work to be much more than a job, people who will stand by the children in their charge at all times, no matter what happens.

Over the years she has spent in Aldeas, Lorena has had four educators. With each of them she has seen a different model of how to educate. The positive thing about this is that in the future she will be in a position to choose the model that best suits her, the one that has worked best for her and the one that she thinks will work best with her children. The truth is she sounds very convincing...

Remembering stories from this period, Lorena describes to me how in moments of rebellion she even planned how to escape, though she never did so. She tells me about a time she broke a light and was punished severely for it when repairing it was easy; it seems that this episode marked her and, despite the passing of time, she has not forgotten it. For her, it was unfair and she continues to proclaim her innocence. We laugh a little, and the tension passes...

Studying, a path to independence

Five years after being taken into Aldeas Infantiles SOS, in the summer of 2000, Lorena had her first contact with the Youth House run by the same organisation. Some time earlier her sister had moved there. This was a time for her to experience what it was like living in a different setting, with other people of her own age. During the months of July and August she took classes to strengthen her computer skills and her English, and lived with the other people in the Youth House. Though it did not seem to her a bad experience, Lorena preferred to go back to her brothers and sisters in the Aldea, for she felt it was still her duty to be with them.

Finally she left to live in the Youth House in September 2001 – the time had come for her to move on, though she would have preferred to avoid it. She had grown up by now and she had to learn to share her life with other young people and leave space in the house for other smaller children. Once she had settled into the Youth House, she adapted very well, and her performance at school improved. She did everything that was expected of her and her attitude was very positive. The worst thing was, she explains, being physically separated from her brothers and sisters. It hurt her and it hurt them.

In early November 2002, at the age of twenty, Lorena left the Youth House and went to live in a semi-independent flat that

Aldeas Infantiles SOS has in Collado Villalba. There, where she is still living at present, she shares the flat with other girls, living almost completely autonomously, though with the support of a team of educators who help them and guide them in whatever way they can. Lorena avoids using the name 'educator', calling them instead 'guides' who visit the flat from time to time to monitor their progress.

In this flat, it is the people who live there who organise the running of their home, the housework – preparing the meals, doing the washing, cleaning, shopping... When I ask her about the day-to-day life there, Lorena tells me that differences sometimes crop up, some arguments, but since there are few of them, it is easier to straighten things out. In this flat, she tells us – Esperanza, Juan Carlos and me, who also take part in the conversation – she has begun to discover, and to feel, what it will be like to live completely independently once she has found a job and can support herself without the help of Aldeas Infantiles SOS.

And Lorena is fully aware of how lucky she has been to have found Aldeas Infantiles SOS. Since arriving there, all her material needs have been met, she has not had to deal with any financial limitations, and she has had an enormous range of experiences with very different people. Apart from the affection and warmth of the staff, there she has been able to receive what she considers to be truly fundamental in life: an education. Vanesa, her elder sister, would have liked to study, but she arrived in Aldeas at the age of sixteen and perhaps it was already too late. Moving into Aldeas Infantiles SOS meant, for Lorena, getting down to studying seriously, in a way that was regular and constant, something she had never been able to do before.

Once settled into the Aldea de San Lorenzo de El Escorial, Lorena started studying the sixth year of primary education. When she started the classes, the truth is that things went very badly; she only knew how to read and write. Luckily, in Aldeas they helped her to cope with her schoolwork. There were volunteers and support teachers who went through all her lessons with her when she came back from school, and in this way, Lorena managed to catch up with the children of her own age. Afterwards she went on to the Juan de Herrera secondary school, in the same town. Of this period, she remembers especially the satisfaction she felt when she managed to complete her secondary education; contrary to what she expected, she eventually succeeded in passing everything. Lorena is not ashamed to admit that she cried more than once when she failed a subject, though in the end, by dint of hard work, she managed to pass them all.

During this time at school Lorena never had any problems with her classmates; she didn't see herself, and neither did they see her, as someone different from them because of her family and social situation. In fact, Lorena has more friends from outside Aldeas, people she met in class, than from inside. Many of the young people from Aldeas left school as soon as possible and went out to work, and she lost contact with them.

At present, Lorena is studying to be an Infant Teacher at the University of Segovia. The reasons why she chose this course have already been made clear; she really likes being with children, participating in their education and their upbringing. Lorena sees this decision as being the natural consequence of what she has lived through. She has always known that this is what she wanted to study, though sometimes she felt disorientated. In fact, once she graduates and can work as a teacher, she sees that her job will be a kind of extension of the family role she has had practically all her life.

I ask her to tell me some of the things she has enjoyed most about the course. She describes the placement she did in the third year, with primary school children around six years old; they are little animals, she says laughing, and they are really hard to control, but the effort is worthwhile. In fact Lorena has been studying to work as an infant teacher, but thanks to the placement she has realised that what she really enjoys is primary education. She'll have to do something about that...

However, the truth is that Lorena would have preferred to study psychology but her marks in 'Selectividad' (the pre-university exam) were not high enough. Her plans are that, when she finishes her teacher training, she will do a bridge course that will allow her to do two years of psychology. Her interest in doing this, she explains, has more to do with personal enrichment than the idea of working as a professional psychologist, though if, one day, it turned out to be possible to do so, what better?

But, first things first. Now the important thing is to finish her present university course and once she has graduated, to find a job, though she is not too clear what she will end up doing.

Lorena would like to combine her work with some of her hobbies. She doesn't want to be a slave to work; just the contrary, she wants to have time to go on holiday, to go to the theatre, to read, to go to the cinema... To be working all the time doesn't appeal to her in the least, since the quality of life is important for her. No matter what happens, whatever she does, Lorena says that she will always have the unconditional support of her mother.

Yet although Lorena likes so many things, what is really important for her are her brothers and sisters. She knows that from time to time she ought to be a little more selfish and look out for her own interests, but she feels better like this, she can't help it; her brothers and sisters are like her own children, she will always put them first, she will always try to look after and protect them.

Speaking about the future

Starting work will mean leaving behind the student life, a life that she loves – why not admit it? Lorena recognises that studying, though it may sometimes be tiring and stressful, is something she enjoys. She has had a lot of fun during the course, more than when she was studying for her '*Bachillerato*' (the Baccalaureate exam, roughly equivalent to British A levels) in Humanities and Social Sciences, a time that was not very easy for her. She has had a really good time at university; even though she has had to burn the midnight oil, she doesn't mind, for it is studying that she really likes.

She tells me, more relaxed now, that, given what she has seen during the summers she has worked, student life is better than a working life. We laugh at the obviousness of this. Since she is a good student, she has been able to spend the summer months working to save some money. She first worked in a large supermarket, stacking shelves. She didn't enjoy it very much since she found the work monotonous and because she had no contact with anybody else.

A job she did enjoy was the one she had last summer in the maternity home that is part of the Aldea de San Lorenzo de El Escorial. There she spent all her time surrounded by children: from babies to youngsters of two and a half years old. She was practising. When she arrived home, she always had to explain what had happened during the day. She felt terrible whenever one of the babies got ill. In general this work experience was very positive and best of all was the fact that her colleagues felt very comfortable working with her.

Now, during the academic year, she gives private classes to children who are having difficulties with primary education – her speciality; she doesn't accept classes with older children. We spoke a little about the situation in schools at present; I give her my opinion and she gives me hers. Parents are never at home, she says, and can't explain the exercises to their children, so this is what she is called in to do. She gives classes every day and, though she reduces her prices a little for those who attend five days a week, she makes a tidy sum by the end of the month. For her, more than a financial motivation, this work gives her a lot of personal satisfaction.

But apart from working and studying, Lorena has also had time for her hobbies, especially for travelling. Paris and Granada are the destinations she has visited, and next will be Prague. Travelling, in addition to being something she likes, also allows her to see different things, different worlds. Lorena also loves reading – much more than music, she tells me. She likes listening to music, but only for a while – she would rather get stuck into a book. She remembers that once, when she was at secondary school, she did some classes in ballroom dancing. She enjoyed it and tried to continue it back at Aldeas, but it wasn't possible.

Talking about the more or less immediate future, Lorena tells me that she sees herself completing, sooner or later, the psychology course. Having her own home, a job, and children, all form part of her desire to create the stability she never knew as a child. On the other hand, she is aware how difficult it is for the young people of today to make their dreams come true, especially in the world of work, something which she sees as essential in order to be able to do many other things. However, she tells me she has no plans to return to Cuenca; everybody in her neighbourhood knows her and she has no desire to be the centre of attention, whether for good or for bad reasons.

With everything that has happened, Lorena feels very proud of herself because she has done her best, and done everything she has set herself to do. What seems best of all to me is that she believes that she has done it all quite well, even though she has had to work very hard. I ask her if she has fulfilled her childhood dreams and, to my surprise, she answers that she didn't dream as a child. She only started to do so when she was already in Aldeas, something that developed as she grew up. Then, her main dream was to study something, and this dream has already come true.

For Lorena, Aldeas Infantiles SOS is the place in which both she and other children have managed to make their dreams come true. The biggest of these was, perhaps, that of being able to be together with her family, with all her brothers and sisters, to maintain the bond with them, and together they have achieved this.

I can see no better end for our conversation. Luckily, Lorena continues to have many dreams and expectations for her future. My dream for her is that she never stops dreaming.

ESPERANZA: DREAMS THAT TRANSCEND BORDERS

Equatorial Guinea, a former Spanish colony, is one of the smallest countries in Africa, on the Atlantic coast, just to the south of Cameroon. Despite a certain national prosperity generated mainly by the recently discovered reserves of oil, the current situation of the population is precarious. This can be seen in the high levels of infant mortality, short life expectancy, high unemployment and illiteracy.

It was into this context that, some twenty-three years ago, Esperanza was born. I am introduced to her in Madrid, in the headquarters of Aldeas Infantiles SOS, in the company of Lorena and Juan Carlos. Of the three, it is she who from the very beginning appears the most open. Two kisses, the exchange of the ritual phrases and we head off to an office in which for the next two hours we will be able to talk freely and calmly. Outside, it is a late June afternoon with a temperature of more than 35ºC; inside, the invaluable air conditioning which swiftly relaxes us all.

Between two continents

Our heroine, Esperanza Carvalho Lomopua, is the seventh in a family of nine brothers and sisters, two of whom, she tells us, have spent time in prison because of their opposition to the dictatorship. At present, as it has been for the last eight years, Esperanza's home is in Spain, in El Escorial (Madrid).

Her arrival at the Madrid Aldea was for very different reasons from those of the majority of boys and girls who are taken in there. With a firm voice, she makes sure that this is made clear from the very beginning. In Equatorial Guinea she lived in a very happy family, where she was treated with great affection by both her parents and her brothers and sisters and where, in material terms, they lacked for very little. What brought her here was a matter of vital importance: her health.

Esperanza arrived in Aldeas in September 1998 in search of a cure for the illness that affected her, scoliosis, lateral curvature of the spine. An aid agreement that exists between Spain and Equatorial Guinea meant that Esperanza, like many other children, was able to travel here to be cured. Once she had recovered, in theory she would return to her family. However theories very often end up being just that, theories, and this was one of those occasions. It is difficult for me to ask her about this, I don't want to embarrass her or be disrespectful but, as we talk more, things come out spontaneously.

In principle, Esperanza was to remain here for three months, time for her to be treated in the hospital where she was to be operated on. This waiting time, however, for various reasons, got longer and longer so, in the end, it was necessary to enrol her in a school so that she did not miss out on too much of her education. Thus, Esperanza was admitted to the 'Colegio de las Monjas Concepcionistas' in San Lorenzo de El Escorial, the 'Conchas', as she fondly calls them.

After the longed-for operation, which unfortunately did not go as well as expected, Esperanza returned home, to her family in

Equatorial Guinea, who were waiting for her with open arms. In her home country, however, she could not receive the medical attention she needed after the operation. The lack of a rehabilitation service and the fact that, periodically, the orthopaedic appliances she had been fitted with needed changing, something that was almost impossible in Guinea, meant that she had to return to Spain in order not to lose the little benefit she had gained by being operated on.

In one of the operations, Esperanza had the misfortune to be left temporarily paraplegic. While undergoing the tough programme of rehabilitation she had to submit to, she decided to remain in Spain, since here there was a much better chance that she would recover her health. It was then that she was told for the first time of Aldeas Infantiles SOS, an institution that, naturally, she had never heard of before. To make it easier for her to understand, they described Aldeas as a group of houses in which there were other children of her age, with people who would look after her and where she would have a really good time. She liked the idea of getting to know a different culture. The idea seemed a good one and so she accepted straight away.

Looking back some years later, Esperanza now sees that her age at that time was an advantage. Being fourteen helped her to understand what was happening to her. She thinks that if she had been younger when she entered Aldeas, despite speaking Spanish, it would have been much more difficult for her to adapt, far away from her loved ones and from the landscapes of her childhood. However, there are times when we feel down and, even though she understood she was in Spain for her own good, Esperanza had many sad days, days when she missed her life with her family.

Ticket to a new life

Thus, what was supposed to be a short stay, in fact lasted years, so much so that Esperanza has ended up making her life in Spain. It is an experience she values for what it has meant to her in all senses, especially in the personal and intellectual fields. Everything she has lived through away from her own country and the protection of her family, especially the difficulties she has had to overcome in terms of her health, has made her stronger, richer as a person. After spending just a few minutes with her I realise that this is a young woman with a very strong character, sure of herself. Leaving behind a life in Guinea to live instead in Europe is a very big change, and one that can throw you off balance. Fortunately, Esperanza has always had friends and people around her who have supported her, both morally and materially, whenever she has needed it.

For everything she has lived through since she arrived in Spain, Esperanza feels very proud of herself. She defines this whole process as a story of constantly overcoming obstacles. Compared with others of her age, in Equatorial Guinea or in Spain, she feels herself to be very fortunate in the opportunities she has been given in Aldeas Infantiles SOS and she has tried to make the most of them, as far as it has been possible.

On arriving in Spain, Esperanza began to do the second year of 'ESO' (compulsory secondary education, normally from 12 to 16 years of age). After the operation she missed several school years though she managed to catch up. Though her Bachillerato did not begin very well, she pushed on and managed to pass both years of her Humanities and Social Sciences course; she has always been a good student, she tells me. At present she is studying a Higher Level 'Formación Profesional' (technical, vocational training) module in Audiovisuals, in Television Production to be precise,

in a specialist centre in Madrid, thanks to a grant she was awarded by a member of Aldeas Infantiles SOS.

Once she had completed her Bachillerato, she knew that she
wanted to continue studying, but she wasn't sure what. She thought
about doing a course in Library Sciences, but then she was offered
the chance of studying in the audiovisual centre and was completely
convinced when they showed her round the installations and
explained the work they do there. Without doubt, she recognises,
this was a unique opportunity for her because in her native land
she would never have been able to study this subject. There she
would either have studied law or oil engineering – there wouldn't
have been many other options. Very often our choices are limited
and you just have to put up with it, she says. Now she is very happy
with the decision she took: she loves the world of cinema, of sound
and image, and hopes to be able to work in this field.

Esperanza explains, with an almost professional pride, that
what she is studying is something that, though it might appear
simple, involves a lot of work. Her studies include digital and ana-
logue montage, editing, scriptwriting, live recording... What she
likes most is montage. She explains that, amongst other things, in
the documentary she is making as a practical exercise, she is pro-
ducing a report on the destruction of the environment. The course
is not easy for her; here the level required is much higher than for
ESO and Bachillerato; in the university sphere, she adds, things
get more complicated. Even so she is very happy because, apart
from the knowledge she is gaining, she is meeting loads of new
people, people from other worlds, other circles.

Making a home into her own country
When Esperanza arrived at Aldeas Infantiles SOS, because of

her age she lived in a house with other children and with an educator who was with them twenty-four hours a day. There, just like in a conventional family, everyone had their own jobs to do around the house, apart from going to class, and all under the supervision of an educator who, for the children, could come to take on the role of a mother – indeed there were some children who called her just that, she adds.

At this moment, the conversation takes on a different tone; an Esperanza with very strong principles, holding fast to her own ideas, appears. Speaking about this initial period in Aldeas, she tells me that she has always been wary of becoming too affectionate towards the educators. I am surprised by this comment, but as if she had read my thoughts, Esperanza tells me she has had very good 'mothers'. She is happy because they didn't punish her much; she is a very good girl, she says, half seriously, half joking, but sometimes the wild beast inside comes out. And I believe her.

Of this first period she also remembers the wariness with which she explained to others – friends or classmates – that she was from Aldeas Infantiles SOS. The fact that there were some problem children meant that some people thought that all the children living there were the same, and in San Lorenzo de El Escorial everybody knows everybody else; so, if they didn't ask her, she didn't say. Esperanza thinks that the problem is that people don't really know what Aldeas is, and that means that situations, and people, can be misinterpreted. Lorena and Juan Carlos, who are also participating in our conversation, agree with her.

Now, since October 2004, Esperanza has been living in supervised accomodation in Monte Escorial, with two other young people from Aldeas. There they live much more independently, and they do practically everything that is necessary to make the flat work; from cooking to washing. However, they also have the support of a person from Aldeas who visits them from time to time to check how they are getting on. In addition, Esperanza combines all these everyday activities with a rehabilitation programme that involves physiotherapy and swimming.

The truth is that Esperanza feels very happy here, above all, because the other girls she shares the flat with are the same age as her and have similar interests. When she was offered the chance to live there, the idea sounded very attractive and she didn't think twice. When you are eighteen, she says, you don't really want to be with smaller children, you want to be getting on with your own life. Though all changes bring with them a certain nervousness, Esperanza faced up to this new stage in her life with energy and enthusiasm.

I ask her to describe a normal day, a working day. It is very full. She gets up and has breakfast; then there is a forty-five minute bus journey from San Lorenzo to Madrid – if there aren't any hold-ups; then half an hour by metro; she goes to the centre where she is studying and when the classes are over, she returns home. Once there, she has to cook, do the shopping or other housework, and then, finally, she gets down to studying.

When it comes to going out with her friends she prefers to wait for the weekend. She says she has more friends in Madrid than in San Lorenzo de El Escorial. In the capital she also has some relatives, from both her mother's and her father's families, who she spends some time with. Life is strange sometimes – she met them for the first time in Spain. She tells me, laughing, that she met a cousin of hers by chance, at a party. The cousin recognised her because she had seen her in some photos they had at home. Truth, I think to myself, is always stranger than fiction.

Apart from her social life, when she is alone at home Esperanza loves listening to music – of all kinds, except 'house' and 'bacalao', she says. For Esperanza, music is an attitude that affects every aspect of your life: the way you dress, the way you dance, the way you are with people... The spirit of music comes from inside you, you can't learn it, either you have it or you don't. The way she is dressed on the day of our meeting reveals a dynamic young woman, restless, absolutely up-to-date.

The journey as an initiation into life

Life in Aldeas, comments Esperanza, is very pleasant. She is aware that, apart from having all her material needs covered, thanks to Aldeas Infantiles SOS she has been able to get to know another culture, another way of life she had never experienced before, something that, in her country, very few people of her age can do. She is profoundly grateful for all that she has been given. In addition, she says jokingly, she has been able to learn another kind of Spanish; the language spoken in Guinea has an intonation and a vocabulary that is a little different from that spoken here. The fact that when she arrived, she spoke a little more slowly than is usual amongst Spanish Castilian speakers was something that initially surprised the other children at Aldeas – Lorena nods. But her way of speaking did not surprise them as much as her thick head of hair, which on the day of the interview, was hidden by a white cap.

When asked about her future, Esperanza shows just how practical she is. The first thing she wants to do is finish her Production course with as good a mark as possible and find a job. But she already knows what the job market is like. She tells me that competition for the best jobs is getting stiffer and stiffer, there being more and more highly qualified people. If, for whatever reason, you turn down a job, there will be plenty of others willing to do it and even willing to accept it for a lower salary. She is very realistic, and in the world of work this is almost essential. If she can't find a job in what she has trained for, she would be prepared to take anything she can get. She doesn't rule out doing a secretarial course so she can get some kind of office work; the more options you have, the better, she thinks.

When I ask her what she wanted to be when she was younger she says that she dreamed of being a famous businesswoman. Now, she adds, the only thing she wants is to find a job in which she feels happy – something which is not easy. But that doesn't mean she isn't ambitious; she thinks it's a good thing to be, especially if the things you are striving for will be beneficial for you. She believes that to achieve this, hard work and drive are basic and fundamental: the more you do, she declares, the more you will be able to achieve. Esperanza does not ask much in professional terms and hopes that, sooner rather than later, her wishes will come true.

She doesn't see herself returning to Guinea; she knows that it would not be a good idea, for her health and because of the political situation in the country. So she expects to stay in Spain and continue her life here. She hopes that when it comes to buying her own home, something almost everybody dreams of doing, the property market will be a little easier and that she will be able to do so at a reasonable price. Meanwhile, she will continue to pay rent, like the enormous majority of young people.

Now feeling a little more confident, I decide to raise the question of her physical health. Here Esperanza shows herself to be even more realistic and pragmatic. I am surprised by the way in which she describes her situation and the misfortune she had with some of the treatments that were supposed to improve the scoliosis she was suffering from. As a girl, the news that she might end up paraplegic took her by complete surprise. Fortunately she managed to recover; first with the help of a wheelchair, now only with the aid of a single crutch and orthopaedic footwear, which she hopes to be able to stop using sooner or later. Before the ill-fated operation she could do some sports – basketball, football, athletics... Now that her life has taken this turn, the only thing she is left with are her sessions in the gym. The fact is that Esperanza is in a rather delicate situation. The doctors can not touch her spine again; if they did, there is a risk that she would end up irremediably tetraplegic. Anybody who listens to her is staggered by the matter-of-fact calmness with which she describes her situation; she has learnt to live with it and she dismisses it, in her way.

In terms of her personal life, at the moment she doesn't see herself getting married in the near future. Despite everything, she says she would like to have a couple of children; she wants to bring them up to value what they have, she wants them to learn to appreciate what they have come to possess through blood, sweat and tears. Family is very important for Esperanza. Though hers is thousands of kilometres from San Lorenzo de El Escorial, they are always with her in her heart. Every so often, when she can, she goes on holiday to Equatorial Guinea to be with them. For them to come and visit her in Spain is much more complicated. Though she can't see them as often as she would like, they frequently phone each other, though it's not the same, she laments. From home, from a distance, they encourage her in everything she does. They are very proud of her and of everything she is achieving, though, obviously, they wish she was there with them.

A bridge between two cultures

Though Esperanza carries in her heart both her family and her homeland, I would go so far as to say that there is not much left of that little girl who arrived at Aldeas Infantiles SOS almost a decade ago. She has adapted completely to the Spanish rhythm of life and way of doing things. However, she still preserves some things from her native Africa. This you can see in her fondness for plaited hairstyles, veritable works of art she creates with her hair and with that of her friends, and that, from time to time, help her to earn a little extra money in her spare time. The timinis, she tells me, are the plaits that lie flat against the head. Plaiting hair, something that can take from just a few minutes to several hours, has become one of her hobbies here; in Guinea, on the other hand, it was almost an obligation whenever she went out onto the street or to school.

I leave Esperanza in the metro, at the Arturo Soria station. Before going home, she has to run a couple of errands. I thank her for the directions she gives me so that I can get back to the centre of Madrid as quickly as possible. I say goodbye but not before wishing her good luck with her life, but then I think she doesn't need that: she has enough resources to get on without having to rely on luck.

JUAN CARLOS: THE ART OF BUILDING DREAMS

The work of an architect, though those of us who know little about the subject sometimes tend to forget this, goes far beyond simply designing façades. From the foundations to the roof, including the whole system of columns and beams, the goal of the architect is to ensure a perfect system that allows the building to stay on its feet. Just as with human beings, the beauty of a building is often to be found in its interior.

To live is simply to gradually construct our own edifice, whether that be a small cottage or a towering skyscraper. The important thing is to carry on building, always adding a little bit more. During the construction, as important as building it up from the ground is ensuring that there are solid foundations, a perfect base on which to be able to stand the future architectural work. Without this element, so essential, there is little that can be done. Without the right support, the whole structure will sooner or later collapse.

I meet Juan Carlos in Madrid. I find him sitting in the reception of Aldeas Infantiles SOS, accompanied by Lorena and Esperanza. Dressed informally, piercings included, from the very outset he seems to be just like any other young man of his age. I wonder if he is shy or serious. I am soon to find out.

Learning in university, and from life

For the last two years, Juan Carlos Pérez León has been studying in the Faculty of Architecture in Madrid. A team of lecturers are charged with teaching him, and many others, all the secrets of this ancient and indispensable art. Perhaps Juan Carlos has still not mastered certain laws of physics or arithmetical calculations; no problem, these he will learn. What they will not need to teach him, of that we can be quite sure, is how to construct a life; Juan Carlos knows perfectly well how to do this, for he might say that since he was very young he has had to do just that, to build his own life.

The conversation I have with him is shared with the two girls. Juan Carlos stays in the background – the girls, it has to be said, dominating our chat. However, when it is his turn, or when he has something to say, he intervenes perfectly. Back at home, listening to the tape on which I recorded the three of them, I realise that he had spoken, and said, much more than I thought. Fantastic!

Juan Carlos was born and brought up in Villanueva de la Jara, a small village in the south of the Province of Cuenca, where he lived with his two younger brothers, José and Samuel. Very early on, the three of them had to go and live with their grandparents. Their parents, to make ends meet, had to work as seasonal labourers in various parts of the peninsula: in Sagunto, for example, they picked oranges. Though the three brothers were split up between their maternal and paternal grandparents – Juan Carlos tells me that he lived with his maternal grandmother, they stayed close, since they all lived in the same village and they almost always ate together.

As a child, Juan Carlos went to three different schools; first in Villanueva, then to a state school in Cuenca – which he really liked, he remembers– and later to a religious school. As the years went by, their grandparents fell ill, and the social and financial situation of Juan Carlos and his brothers worsened. Thus it was that, in 1997, the three of them were admitted to Aldeas Infantiles SOS in Cuenca under a voluntary custody order at the request of their parents, conscious as they were that for the moment they could not look after them.

At just ten years of age, Juan Carlos was taken into the Aldea in Cuenca, where he was able to continue living with his two brothers. He remembers that time as one of the saddest periods of his life; naturally, he didn't like being separated from his family, from his childhood friends and the landscapes amongst which he had grown up. He had been very happy in the village and, being so young, he couldn't understand why he had been taken away from there. Though they told him that it was a place where he would be able to study and be with other children of his own age, until his parents managed to stabilise their financial situation, Juan Carlos at that time felt it was much more important for him to be able to stay with his family; studying was of secondary importance. I suppose we all would have felt the same.

Nevertheless, Juan Carlos managed to adapt to this new life.

His parents never managed to set the family finances on an even keel and the three brothers ended up having to stay in Aldeas Infantiles SOS much longer than was originally thought. Now, years later, Juan Carlos recognises that the negative aspects of being separated from his family went hand in hand with many other positive things, like the one they had promised him – the possibility of studying. In the village, the most he could have aspired to, given his personal circumstances, was completing his basic education and then going out to work. In Aldeas, however, he was given the chance and, above all, the necessary facilities to continue with his studies right up to university level. Juan Carlos, now, sees that he has been fortunate, he has been given the opportunity of having a better future, and that, I think, doesn't happen to everybody.

Juan Carlos' relationships with the different educators have varied, though overall the balance is positive. Suddenly, he comes out with a thought about this. With hindsight, and from a certain distance, he begins, he is aware now of how hard it must be to be an educator in Aldeas Infantiles SOS – long hours of work and children who, in principle, want nothing more than to play and have fun. Though in theory they have two days off a week, Juan Carlos continues, they work many more hours than they are supposed to do, and if on top of all that, they have a group like his, a bit rowdy and misbehaved, then things are even more complicated. You've got to be really committed..., he says with a playful smile. And he confesses that during those first years in Aldeas he and his friends often played up, to the point that they exhausted the patience of the people who were working with them. Though they were only childish pranks, from time to time they got into real trouble. But later, as time passed, Juan Carlos calmed down a bit, straightened himself out, and ended up getting on really well with everyone.

In 2003, at the age of eighteen, he moved to the Youth House, where he stayed until August 2004. Since then, Juan Carlos has been part of the Autonomy Programme of Aldeas, from whom he receives the financial support necessary to cover his expenses as a university student. Unlike the other boys he studied with in Villanueva de la Jara and those he lived with in Aldeas, Juan Carlos decided to continue studying and go on to university. By the way he says this, I understand that this was something he had thought about a lot.

In this important decision his family supported him, just as they had always urged him that studying was the best thing he could do with his life. The people at Aldeas were obviously of the same mind. Juan Carlos weighed up the pros and cons and came to the conclusion that his future lay in studying.

During the final year of his Bachillerato Juan Carlos knew that he wanted to study architecture, a course that, as he points out, is not for poor people, in the sense that the materials you need to do the course are very costly. With help from Aldeas Infantiles SOS and from the grants he receives from the Government of Castilla-La Mancha and the Ministry of Education (the latter far from easy to obtain, since every year it is necessary to obtain a certain level of marks in order to receive it the following year), two years ago he was able to begin adding another storey to the building that is his life.

High quality property with outstanding finishes

Today Juan Carlos has left Cuenca to live in Madrid, very near to the Faculty. He is living in the Colegio Mayor Marqués de la Ensenada, a university Hall of Residence just five minutes from where he studies, and so he is able to avoid the daily traffic jams that plague this great city – something that the people of Madrid have learnt to live with – and the rush-hour crowds on the metro. Life in this student residence is relatively easy; he doesn't have to worry about shopping, cooking or other household chores. As he says, everything is done for him and he even has time to take a siesta.

If, some years ago, someone had told him that he would now be living in the capital, in a Hall of Residence, studying to be an architect, he wouldn't have believed them, and more so bearing in mind that when he was younger he wanted to be a policeman. Now Juan Carlos has other heroes, all of them flesh and blood, but also creators of magnificent buildings. The Swiss Le Corbusier, the German Mies van der Rohe, exponents of the best rationalist architecture, or the Spaniard Rafael Moneo, author amongst other works of the Museum of Roman Art in Mérida, are just some of the great architects Juan Carlos admires and would love to emulate in the future.

In the residence, Juan Carlos has all the time in the world, and even then it's not enough, to devote himself to his architecture studies. Many sleepless nights, sketching endlessly and finishing the projects or other models he has to make, or revising mathematics or other subjects. In the faculty, he tells me, they have made him discover his taste for drawing; he never imagined he could draw as well as he does now. Juan Carlos considers himself to be a good student, he always has been. However, now, in the faculty, as is only to be expected, he finds it a little more difficult. There is much more work to do – it's nothing like the secondary school. In the first year he passed all the subjects, but in the second, things are proving to be a little more complicated.

Even though it might appear otherwise, Juan Carlos is no swot; he is not the typical student who shuts himself up all weekend. He knows that there is a time for everything – for studying, but also for having fun. Whenever he can, he does some sport, which helps him to unwind a little from his studies. He likes all sports, especially those that involve some risk. He also really likes music, to the extent that he has learnt to play the electric guitar. In fact he has always enjoyed playing instruments; with a nun who worked at Aldeas he used to play the Spanish guitar, playing all kinds of religious songs, he explains, half embarrassed, half blushing with pleasure. Now, obviously, he prefers other kinds of music, a little more alternative. From time to time he likes to go to music festivals or concerts, like Viña Rock, where he can listen to high quality music.

For Juan Carlos music fills him – it's a way of life. Travelling is another of his passions. He has visited France, Belgium, England and Holland, though he has also explored the peninsula – Torrevieja, Roda de Barà, Barcelona... He especially remembers the Camino de Santiago, a journey he made with others from Aldeas Infantiles SOS. They walked 170 km, from O Cebreiro to Santiago de Compostela, a trip he will never forget. Carrying their rucksacks and sleeping wherever they could were some of the hardest things about the expedition, but it was all worth it once they reached their goal. His expression, serious during much of our conversation, relaxes and his eyes light up as he describes amusing incidents from the past.

Returning to the university, he explains that he will very probably leave the Hall of Residence soon to share a flat with other friends to try and get even more out of his student life. He is not particularly worried about this step, even though it will mean losing some of the comforts he currently enjoys. In fact in Aldeas, apart from learning how to keep house – from cooking to doing the washing – he has learnt one of the most important things in life: how to live with other people. This is one of the advantages he has over other young men of his age.

Large windows with unbeatable views
Not long from now Juan Carlos sees himself finishing his course,

especially the project that, once completed, will allow him to graduate as a fully-fledged architect. What Juan Carlos wants, once his university life is over, is to work. In fact, he says, many students find work in the studios and offices of architects in the city before they even graduate.

He explains that now, in architecture, they train you to work in many fields – students no longer specialise as they did before, and so he does not know exactly what he will end up doing within the discipline. Though he would like to stay and work in Spain he wouldn't mind spending some time abroad to complete his studies. He admits with resignation that he will live wherever he finds work, without showing signs of any particular preference for one place or another. What he is very clear about is that, when he finishes, he does not intend to continue studying. For the moment he has quite enough with a degree in architecture, though a Master's could always come in handy. But it's important not to let things get on top of you, he feels it's time for a break.

So far Juan Carlos has worked some summers to make a little money and to have a bit extra for his personal expenses. Easter and the summer, with the arrival of the tourists, are good times for young people to find work in Cuenca. There, Juan Carlos has worked as a waiter in a bar in the very busy Plaza Mayor, and in a typical meson restaurant, serving beer. He enjoyed the experience, met a lot of people, and on top of that made a bit of money for his savings and for the things that take his fancy.

Quality materials
Despite his student life in Madrid, Juan Carlos still keeps contact with Cuenca and Villanueva de la Jara. When he has a holiday, on Bank Holidays or at weekends, he goes back to Cuenca.

Once there he meets up with his lifelong friends, both with those he met through Aldeas and with former school friends. His relationship with other lads, even though they know that he was in Aldeas, has never given him any kind of problem, just the opposite, it has made things even better, he says. At summer camps or on other occasions, he has always explained where he is from, but only when a good opportunity to do so has arisen. People tend to be a bit put off at first, but afterwards they react well and are pleasantly surprised by him. Juan Carlos is a young man who is very likeable, appealing to both his friends and to their parents – it's not difficult to see why. Sometimes he feels that he is part of their families: they ask him to stay the night, they invite him out to eat… He feels proud of that and comments to us that some of his friends and their families have become members of Aldeas after hearing his story.

When he goes to Cuenca, Juan Carlos also makes time to go and visit his family. The relationship he has with them, with his parents, his only surviving grandfather and his uncles and aunts, is quite good. In fact, it always has been, despite the ups and downs they have been through. Nevertheless, Juan Carlos admits that both he and his parents have, with the passing of time, made different lives for themselves, each going their own way. Though this might seem a sad thing to say, Juan Carlos says it with confidence and firmness, without any kind of affectation.

The family, he says, is the most important thing for him. Though at the moment it's difficult for him to imagine himself with a wife and children, one of his dreams is that his kids will lack for nothing. But he is not talking so much about material goods as about the values and principles he has learnt over the years. Years in which, little by little, he has bettered himself, setting himself goals that with his hard work, and with the help of Aldeas Infantiles SOS, he has managed to fulfil. Juan Carlos sees his life as a path along which every period has brought its obstacles, both personal and social, that he has had to overcome. His next challenge is to turn himself into an architect; in the long term, he will, I am sure, place a fine roof atop this magnificent building that he has built with such tenacity and patience.

Once our chat was over, the four of us headed out into the street towards the metro. Mauricio, our photographer, took advantage of the moment to take even more photos. Juan Carlos appears stiff – having your photo taken by a complete stranger is a bit intimidating. I try to relax him a bit by chatting to him about contemporary architecture. I invite him to come to Barcelona and see the city's modern buildings; he, today, has taught me a lot of things and I want to give him something in return.

MAMEN, *MENS SANA IN CORPORE SANO*; GOOD ON THE OUTSIDE, EVEN BETTER WITHIN!

In Ancient Times they had a saying: mens sana in corpore sano- 'a healthy mind in a healthy body'. The cult of the body has led to the appearance of gyms in every town and city in Spain and people now take much more care of their appearance than ever before.

But what is more complicated, I think, is how to deal with inner beauty or, what in the end comes to the same thing, the calmness of soul and spirit. The pace of modern everyday life produces stress, overwhelms or depresses us. We all have to deal with this at some point in our lives. Progress brings an improvement in the quality of life in some respects, but just the opposite in others.

Our next protagonist, Carmen Lorite Tapia, known by one and all as Mamen, knows everything there is to know about the cult of the body, for she takes the greatest pains to look after her physique. Mamen, who says she is not in the least vain, does not much like wearing make-up; she prefers to show herself as nature made her. However, she works very hard to build up and strengthen her muscles, muscles that would certainly do credit to a top sportswoman, something that confirms, though she would never admit it, the coquettish side to her. In her words, Mamen idolises her body. For her there is nothing she likes more than keeping herself in shape, so she does all kinds of sports – football, basketball, swimming... to keep herself fit and healthy.

Everything I've said so far is immediately obvious when you meet Mamen, when you see her face to face. A face that is completely clean – without make-up, I mean – her hair hanging loose, and her simple, comfortable clothes, all speak of the naturalness of this young woman; a naturalness that is evident in both her body and her mind. Though so much attention to her body might appear excessive, after speaking to Mamen you realise that this is her way of declaring to the world that she values her life, both on the outside and on the inside. For Mamen, despite her tender years, takes great care that her mind and her spirit can breathe calmly. She has been through so much that now it's time to relax a little, to take a pause in her personal marathon to regain her breath.

Before the race

I am introduced to Mamen for the first time in the company of two other young women, Inma Figueredo and Rubí, two friends of hers and companions from Aldeas Infantiles SOS. Our meeting takes place in a house that the organisation has near Avenida Arturo Soria in Madrid. My aim is to talk to them, to chat during the few hours I have before returning to Barcelona. Fernando, a worker with Aldeas, tells them that the interview is going to be published in one of the top fashion magazines in the country; that they should make themselves look good, because the photos are bound to be on the front cover... Fernando, who knows them well, eases them into the situation with his jokes. He breaks through the girls' shyness, which, after barely five minutes of conversation, has disappeared completely.

Mamen Lorite Tapia was born twenty years ago in Linares, an important commercial and industrial centre in the Province of Jaén. Many will doubtless know this Andalusian town as being the birthplace of Andrés Segovia, a virtuoso on the Spanish guitar; from now on, I would ask you to remember it as also being the birthplace of Mamen.

Joking aside, fate led Mamen to be born into a family with serious social and financial problems related to drugs, and in which prostitution provided the only source of income. In addition, her mother was incapable of looking after her children, who came from different relationships. She was unable to give them the love and education they needed and, even less so, the financial security. Obviously, as can only be too easily imagined, a life such as this on the edge of society was hardly the best setting for the five children to grow up in or develop adequately.

Mamen arrived at Aldeas Infantiles SOS in Granada when she was just three years old. She went there from the San José de las Montañas Centre, in Marmolejo, where she had been taken in under a neglect ruling. At first, little Mamen lived in Aldeas with all her brothers and sisters but, at a particular moment, three of them left. Mamen tells me that she didn't like this at all, since she would have preferred all of them to stay together; she misses them a lot but, as she says in a very serious voice, sometimes these things are inevitable, and we have no option but to keep going. So, she was left alone with her sister, her much-loved Loles, her last connection with the family she was born into.

Now, when all this seems so long ago, Mamen continues in one of the houses Aldeas Infantiles SOS has in Granada and in which she has lived seventeen years of her life. She lives with her biological sister and with three others she is not biologically related to, though it is as if she were. Being there, growing up in this setting, has meant a lot to her and she is profoundly grateful; she says it in so many words, but you can also detect this in the way that she speaks, and you can see it in her eyes.

You might say that Mamen has spent her whole life in Aldeas Infantiles SOS; though her relationship with her biological family was quite close, Mamen knows no other family setting than that she has lived in Aldeas. There came a moment in which she became aware of herself, something we all go through at some point in our lives, and Mamen realised that she didn't want to live the sad little panorama in which her biological family were living. And so, little by little, she has broken away from this and chosen her own path through life, a path on which she has been guided, helped and encouraged by the people at Aldeas Infantiles SOS. This decision, it should come as no surprise, did not bring out the best in her mother who did not like the idea that her daughter, so young, had already decided with whom, how and where she wanted to grow up. "They've brain-washed you", she told her, but Mamen knew very well what she wanted. It was a very hard moment. With time, the pain of this episode will begin to fade...

The best trainer, the best training of all

As Mamen herself explains, it was in Aldeas Infantiles SOS that she met the woman who for many years has been a mother to her and who, it must be said, she now considers to be her real mother. The educator who tiny Mamen met when she arrived in Granada has taught her almost everything she knows in life, especially everything to do with personal growth and living with others. Remembering the years she has spent in Aldeas, she has no complaints at all. She says that this is what her life has been and it hasn't been at all bad. She recognises that over the years, despite the difficult situation her family have been going through, things have gone very well for her; though there have been bad times, she only wants to remember the best, the most emotive.

Though Mamen appears to be a serious girl, sometimes with a worried look on her face, inside she guards a highly positive, optimistic spirit that gives her the strength to keep going in the difficult times. Sitting there in front of me, while the others are talking, I observe her and wonder what she is thinking, what's going on in her mind…

Mamen also recognises the role that Aldeas Infantiles SOS has played in her intellectual development. There they have always stressed to her the importance of education if you want to make something of yourself in life, to lay the foundations for a good future; she has taken note of this. In this respect, she points out that one of the things they have laid most emphasis on is that it's not the result that counts, but the work you put in. This carries with it a strong sense of bettering yourself, an aspect she values very highly. This is evident in the emphatic tone of voice and in the tense look in her eyes. Mamen knows that she can always give more of herself, that she must never be satisfied with the mini-mum, but always aspire to achieving something more; this is her objective, her goal. She defines herself as a very stubborn person, and when she decides on something, she won't stop until she gets it. A gold medal would be better than a silver…

Though now she sees herself as a good student, hard-working and disciplined, Mamen openly admits that it has not always been like this. When she was small, school went more or less okay, though it was difficult for her to adapt because she was more interested in playing and having fun. Luckily, in Aldeas, when she came home from school they insisted she went though the lessons, that she practised her writing and got her sums right. Now Mamen is very proud of her handwriting, something she worked hard to achieve, and of her regular study habits; both are things she has learnt at Aldeas. At first you might get the impression that Mamen is a 'perfect lady' given the confidence with which she says things; but she can just as easily flatter herself as recognise her faults and defects. She is the first to admit that though she really likes studying, there are times when she gets a bit lax about her work and loses the rhythm a little.

Having left the Cristo Rey School in Granada, at present Mamen is studying Teacher Training, specialising in Physical Education, at the Inmaculada Concepción Teacher Training College in the same city. She chose the course because, as I mentioned earlier, she loves physical exercise and sport in general; in addition, she loves being with children and dealing directly with them. Mamen considers that her university experience to date (she has a year left to do before she finishes) has been very gratifying. You can see it in the glint in her eyes. Once she has finished the course, she explains, she would like to study in the INEF – the National Institute of Physical Education – get the double qualification, and then take the exams to get a permanent teaching place in a state school. The fact is that Mamen is a very restless and ambitious young woman – she never seems to have enough.

Mamen loves the faculty and all the people there, those who work and those who study. She mentions especially her teachers, who she says are very good and very competent. They are people who support her a lot and encourage her to keep studying at every opportunity. It's really good to meet people like this, says Mamen. Apart from the teachers, obviously, there are also all the friendships she has built up during her time there, with both men and women. In this sense, Mamen does not feel in the least bit different because she comes from Aldeas Infantiles SOS. Just the opposite, she sometimes considers herself to be luckier, recognising that she might well have more opportunities than the rest of her fellow students. She is fully aware that, in financial terms, thanks to the unconditional support from Aldeas, she can continue studying. Some of her friends, brought up in conventional families, have to combine their studies with work so as to be able to support themselves. Some have even had to leave off their studying to go and pick olives with their parents, for example.

The final sprint

When Mamen finishes her studies, she is very clear about what she is going to do. She wants to get down to looking for a job and find something steady; and if it is connected with what she has studied, all the better. For her, having a good job and being able to look after herself financially without having to depend on anyone else is vitally important. In this sense she defines herself as being a strong feminist, or rather, that her opinions about this are very radical. Her friends, Inma and Rubí, laugh out loud in unison. They say that Mamen got this from the educator she has had in Aldeas; she doesn't deny it.

When she finds a job, it will not be the first time that Mamen has entered the world of work. When she was seventeen she got a temporary job on a farm in Albera. She has both good and bad memories of this experience but, as is only to be expected with her, she chooses to remember only the former. Another job was in an assembly plant, where she worked for a month and a half as a warehouseman – or woman. There she enjoyed herself more; she could work at her own pace, she says, and nobody was standing over her and telling her what to do. In this job she met many people and, very especially, her boyfriend.

In terms of her university studies, Mamen has done placements with primary school children, something she really enjoyed. Very moved, she describes the work done with a fairly troublesome boy, who they have finally managed to get to apply himself to his schoolwork. From being bottom, he is now one of the top pupils in his class. Though one swallow doesn't make a summer, Mamen feels very proud of this achievement. It has finally convinced her that teaching is what she really wants to do with her life.

At the moment, Mamen doesn't think too much about the future – she prefers to live the present. It's easy to see that she knows very well what her aims are, and exactly what she'll have to do to achieve them. Once she finds a steady job and has saved enough, one of Mamen's dreams would be to get married and raise a family, a family like the one she has known through Aldeas Infantiles SOS, the kind of family she would never have had if it had not been for them. She would love to give her children all she has received and make sure that they never have to go through what she has been through.

When she was younger, Mamen explains, she dreamt constantly of having a family; she pictured herself as a mother, wearing an apron, doing the housework. Nevertheless, with the passing of time she has come to realise that this is not the most fundamental thing in her life. Besides, she adds, half serious, half joking, her man will have to do his share around the house, the chores will be divided between the two of them, with no shame, everybody the same; if we have to draw up a roster – like they do in her Aldeas house – then so be it. However, the most important thing for Mamen is to have somebody near you who loves you, who gives you affection. That's how she feels with her boyfriend. For Mamen it's essential not to feel alone. According to her, this is crucial for her to be able to keep going. The best thing in life is being loved, being helped, she says with conviction. Money is not the first thing, it will always take second place.

The worst thing about growing up, about becoming independent, will be having to leave Aldeas Infantiles SOS, her true home – she has no difficulty admitting it. Mamen would like to stay there for ever, but she knows that is impossible. What she is sure about is that she will try to keep in touch with the organisation – it's what her heart tells her to do, and it's also a recognition of the immense gratitude she feels towards all those who have helped her, listened to her and given her the warmth and affection she needed to be able to lead a dignified life. She has no idea what would have happened to her if she had stayed with her biological family. And these words are spoken very sincerely.

Crossing the finishing line

Mamen doesn't hide the fact, nor is she in the least ashamed of it, that she belongs to the great big family that is Aldeas Infantiles SOS. She assures me she has never had any problem as a result, quite the opposite, everything has been offered to her. When people ask her about herself 'And you, whose child are you?', she explains with gusto, almost as if she was advertising Aldeas: what it is, what she does there, how she lives, and with whom... She even goes as far as insisting that in some senses she has had it much better than other people who were brought up within their biological families. Besides having her financial needs covered, whenever she has had a personal problem there have been people who were prepared to help her, to resolve the dilemma or to help her get over a rough patch. Help that, she says, many other young people of her age have been deprived of.

In other aspects, Mamen is a normal young woman, a young woman of today. She likes pop music, especially black music: singers like Jamelia, Beyoncé or Ashante fill her with passion. In addition, her boyfriend has introduced her to flamenco, music she always plays at home or in the car. She also likes reading, not only fiction but books of any kind. Mamen likes knowing everything and to do so she reads. She also really likes travelling, though she can't do it very often. Instead, she makes do with remembering the good times she has had. For example, during the Aldeas summer camps, with other children, or a camp she went on in Italy. She also lets me in on a small secret: when she was little, she dreamt of being an actress or a dancer.

A place of honour on the podium

Mamen's is another story of striving to better herself, of working from day to day, of overcoming the obstacles that life presents. She knows about her past, she knows that it is there, that she cannot wipe it out, and that it is a past that she doesn't like at all. Yet today, in the present, she is a young woman who feels very proud of herself, something she freely admits – you can tell she likes blowing her own trumpet, she says laughing. She admits that in her life, she has sometimes gone a little astray, she hasn't always taken any notice of what people told her, but she has always managed to react in time.

INMA, FROM *CANTE JONDO* TO *BULERÍAS*

Whether it be as *soleá*, *malagueñas*, *peteneras*, or any of the myriad of others, the art of flamenco takes thousands of forms, depending on who produces it and who listens to it. For Inma Figueredo Rodríguez, flamenco is what she likes best, apart from, it must be said, some men! She and her friends long to get out into some small square in the city and, to the rhythm of clapping hands and voices raised in song, mount a little flamenco festival, for then they forget their everyday woes. For flamenco, 'flamenquillo', as she calls it, forms a much greater part of Inma's life than perhaps even she imagines. To the sad yet brazen 'cante jondo' of her childhood, have been added now the joyful 'sevillanas', the passionate 'copla' and the overflowing energy of the 'tanguillos'.

But much more important is what Inma carries within herself, a spirit reflected in her jet black eyes, something a little mysterious, indescribable, yet that you perceive instantly. Listening to Inma, with her peculiar Andalusian accent, watching the torrent of gesticulations and contemplating her typically Spanish features, is to enjoy a 'duende' – that expressive, emotive and utterly authentic soul which, unruly as it is, never stops, not by day nor by night.

I meet her in Madrid, in one of the Aldeas. Inma has just arrived, together with Rubí and Mamen, after a long journey from Granada. She has arrived tired but, after smartening herself up a bit, very necessary this, for she is very coquettish, she is ready for our chat. I find her sitting on a sofa, watching the beginning of a football match involving the Spanish national team. With the first thing she says I realise that I am going to enjoy myself, enjoy myself a lot. Inma is not one to bite her tongue – she says what she thinks. Frankness first and foremost. I reassure her; I only want to chat with her, to find out something about her life, for her to explain how she got to where she is now. Easy, no?

Difficult beginnings

Inma was born twenty-one years ago in the city of Almería. The family situation in which she spent the first years of her life was not, unfortunately, ideal either for her or for her four brothers and sisters – she is the third of five. As a result of her mother's inability to properly care for, educate and bring up her children, while still very small, they were taken in to the Provincial Children's Home in Almería. Shortly afterwards, in 1989, seeing that the children were suffering from neglect, Inma was taken into a home run by the 'Nuevo Futuro' Association, in the same city. A year later, given that the family's circumstances had not changed, Inma was transferred at barely five years of age to Aldeas Infantiles SOS in Granada. There she was to stay, together with her brother and sister, until she was sixteen.

Inma does not have very good memories of that first period in Aldeas Infantiles SOS. When speaking of that part of her life in Granada, her face saddens and her voice becomes flat, its tone deadened. For, as is only normal, she felt very attached to her mother and didn't want to leave her. I ask her about her father: she answers, unhesitatingly, that she had never known him. Fortunately for her, her brothers and sisters were very close.

Various factors contributed to the fact that Inma did not feel at home in that Aldeas house; it was difficult for her to adapt. It wasn't a question of having to keep to timetables or do housework or any of the other chores that she had never, up until that moment, had to worry about. From what she tells me, I deduce that it was some kind of unconscious rebellion against what she was going through.

A change for the better

When she left the Aldeas home and moved into a shared flat, also part of Aldeas Infantiles SOS, everything changed. The strangest thing, as she remembers it, is that she had always said she wanted to get out of the Aldeas house, and yet when at last they gave her the chance to do just that, she suddenly realised that she was very happy in the Aldea and that she didn't want to leave; she had spent so many years there... It was obviously fear of change, of beginning a new life; the fear of having to face new and unknown things.

Neither should we forget that Inma was going through adolescence at this time. She admits she has always been a bit rebellious, perhaps, as the song says, because life had made her like that. As she puts it, she didn't enjoy her adolescence in Aldeas but now, looking back, it doesn't appear to have been all that bad. She recognises, for example, that some of her best friends are people she met in Aldeas; some of them, having lived together for so many years, are almost like brothers and sisters. The warmth of the friendship and affection between her, Mamen and Rubí, is obvious for all to see.

Inma is currently living in this shared flat, in the La Cartuja area of Granada and, listening to her, I sense that she feels very happy there. She shares it with a young man and another young woman, both of them students. They get along together very well, and they all share the housework. If there is a disagreement or a problem between them, they also have the support of a person from Aldeas who visits them quite often to see how they are getting on. Thanks to one of the educators she had, she explains, she now knows how to cook quite well. If it hadn't been for this woman there would be many things she wouldn't have learnt yet.

As she explains this new stage, one of the most important in her life, her whole face lights up. From the moment she moved in there, her relationship with the educators changed a lot. She didn't have any problems, everything was positive, everything was good. As she puts it, she has had some fantastic teachers, really cool. She went everywhere with them; to eat, to the cinema, to have a drink... In the evenings, she remembers, they used to tell her everything they'd done during the day, their problems, their hopes and fears... But even with the support of these educators, the moment arrived in which Inma began to lead her life more independently. She feels very proud of this. Learning to live in a more independent way made her feel much better, though she knew the people at Aldeas were there if she needed them.

Up until a few years ago, education was one of the areas in which our 'flamenquilla' was not doing very well. As she puts it, as a young girl she was very rebellious and a little lazy; she didn't want to study, she didn't want to do anything... Fortunately, things change with time. As you get older, so you grow up, and you see things from another angle. When Inma had to repeat the first year of her Bachillerato, her life changed radically and she came to understand it was necessary to study; that she had to settle down and change direction. When she is telling me this, I can see that she feels a little embarrassed about it... But being her, she doesn't hide it.

Getting ahead thanks to her studies

Not many of the young people she lived with in Aldeas have decided to continue studying. But she has done just that; she is very sincere, she doesn't much like studying but sees that it is necessary if she wants to get on in life. Though Inma, as she herself is the first to recognise, does not normally listen to the advice she is given – not the good advice, nor the bad – a moment arrived when she saw the light and understood that it would be much better for her to continue with her education. What motivated her to study is that things, life in general, can be very difficult but you always have a better chance if you've got some kind of qualification to fall back on. What is more, her elder sister, Begoña, has always encouraged her to go on studying, to keep fighting, to never give up.

Now she is finishing her second year of a Mid-Level course in Business Administration – something she likes and that, in addition, she has been told will open many doors in the world of work. When she was small, she says, she never thought she would end up studying this. At first it was difficult, because everything was new, and she felt a bit lost, but in this second year she has worked really hard and has managed to pass everything.

Inma knows there is nothing like the life of a student, despite the headaches when exams come round, and no matter how hard she finds it to study when somebody or other in her family is going through a bad time. However, although she would like to continue studying, right now she is keen to finish and find herself a job as soon as possible. At the moment she is sending out CVs; she says she'd like to find a job as an assistant in an estate agent's, in a financial or tax consultancy, or with a building company, as long as it is in Granada. She doesn't want to go back to Almería, even though her family is there, a family that – it must be said – she loves a lot and visits very often. But she knows that her life is now in the city of the Alhambra. Inma does not see her future very clearly yet, but it's something that she is not in the least bit worried about.

Passing her own exam

For Inma is very strong; I tell her this and she denies it. She says she gives the appearance of being a strong, determined young woman, but deep down she is not like that. She says she tries to give the impression of being strong-willed, especially with the exuberance and joviality she transmits, but that in reality she is quite weak. She has no problem admitting she cries a lot, that anything that happens to her or that people say to her affects her a lot; what she doesn't know is that that is not being weak, but sensitive, and sensitivity is part of the duende she carries inside her.

Another of the aspects that Inma is very proud of is the way in which she has managed to get herself back on track. She's well aware that some of the 'friends' she has had might well have misled her and things could have ended up very badly. This bad company might have led her down a blind alley. Many of these friendships went very wrong, she tells me, her voice very serious. Luckily, she knew what she wanted out of life and decided to follow her own path. Besides, she recognises that in Aldeas she has been given very good advice about what would be best for her and, even though it might have seemed that she was not listening, she heard what she needed to... Inma likes to go her own way, to live her life, but she knows how to listen.

Fortunately for her she has many people around her who have helped her to keep going, and to face up to her problems – especially her sister and her boyfriend, naturally another fan of flamenco. Thanks to them she has not felt alone. Her boyfriend, as she explains proudly, has always helped a lot, listening to her and sharing in her decisions. One of her is dreams is to go and live with him, to start a new life together. When she was small, her dream was to live with her mother, something that could not be; now, it is to live with the person she loves and raise a family with him. I really hope this dream comes true for her...

Inma is very much in love – she feels very lucky to have met this man. An enormous smile breaks out whenever she speaks about him – about how good he is, about how he cares for her... A young man who was amazed when Inma explained her life to him: where she came from, how she had been educated and the difficulties she has had to deal with in her life. He understood her very well and the only thing he said was how proud he was of her. When she explains this, the tears well up...

For all these reasons, Inma feels very happy, and it's understandable that she should be. The truth is that she has met many people who have rejected her simply because she is from Aldeas Infantiles SOS. Inma explains this, hurt, with a little resentment, even spite, in her eyes. It is very hard to see people who are supposed to be your friends, the parents of your boyfriends and even teachers at school rejecting you because of where you come from. But this she cannot forget, and despite the years that have gone by, she continues to remember it with sadness. This is why, although she is very open and outspoken, she tends not to talk about her time in Aldeas, and despite being very grateful to the organisation, she always keeps this experience somewhere in the background.

The future – going for it!

When she is asked about her personal future, Inma answers jokingly that within a few years she can imagine herself with a few more wrinkles, as she points out some non-existent crow's feet. For she is very vain; let no-one touch her clothes and make-up! And if she has her photo taken, she asks the photographer to try and not show the mole she has on her nose, which she hates. Joking aside, within a few years Inma imagines herself to be working and living with her partner. Children also appear in these future plans. Twenty-four is the perfect age to be a mother, she claims. I think to myself that that is just round the corner for her, but listening to her talk it seems as if it is still a long time away.

With her children and her man, Inma will be the happiest woman in the world. In this sense, she defines herself as being very traditional, though nowadays it's not very politically correct to admit this. Women, she thinks, have their work to do at home, just as men have theirs. She knows that society is very sexist and in terms of the home, she admits that she is too, though only to a certain extent. She likes thinking about her future home life. She imagines herself shouldering most of the responsibility for the housework, though her partner will have to help her. She is going to be a proper housewife: cooking, cleaning, looking after the household expenses...; she wants to take it all upon herself, even if she has her own job outside the house. No mother-in-law will have to teach her anything, I think, for her time in Aldeas has made her perfectly equipped to run a home...

However, though Inma likes traditional family life, she is very clear that she wants to work. Another of the many things she has learnt during her time in Aldeas, she says adamantly, is that she will never allow herself to be financially dependent on any man. She has to be able to support herself, with her own money, because we never know what life might bring, and circumstances that seem stable now might change in the future. Inma is very clear about this and, in addition, is conscious of just how hard it is for women in the world of work at present. As she says, a woman with no education has it harder than a man in the same situation; much harder. Inma knows many young women who are tied to their partners, even though they don't want to be, for financial reasons. They just don't know where to turn, she says, when their relationships break down. Inma doesn't want the same thing to happen to her.

Meanwhile...

But talking of all this, at the moment, is talking of the future. And until it arrives, Inma continues to enjoy those earthly pleasures she loves so much while still combining them with her studies and her search for work. Firstly, flamenco, especially 'El Bicho', her idol, and favourite artist. But also, showing her more romantic side, Inma declares herself to be a fan of Alejandro Sanz, amongst other singers of ballads. Of the women artists, she plumps for JLo, better known as Jennifer López. She loves her way of singing, dancing, moving, the clothes she wears... She's the best, she declares firmly. But Inma is not far behind la López, claiming to be brilliant at dancing to 'reggaeton'... She dances like you've never seen, man! Another of her pleasures, when she's not with her boyfriend, is going out with her girl friends, having a coffee, gossiping a while, going to the cinema... She loves films – she's seen almost all of them. If she could, she'd love to travel, around Spain and the rest of the world. Inma remembers excitedly a trip to Italy: to Rome, Venice and Florence. She says she hasn't got any hobbies, but I'd bet my life that she never gets bored...

Any pleasure she gets from all this is too little – she deserves more, much more. Inma's life has been a constant battle to improve her lot. She's very aware of just how lucky she's been, especially when she compares herself with some of her companions in Aldeas who have not gone on to study like her. They wanted to go too fast, they were in too much of a hurry, they played at being grown-ups and now they are paying the price. Inma has taken advantage – more or less, she corrects herself – of all the opportunities she has been offered by the organisation. Though she sometimes goes her own way, she has also taken note of the advice she's been given and has managed to choose that which best suits her. She says she is not one for giving advice but, with an almost maternal instinct, Inma is advising her younger brother – who trusts her a lot – to study, not to lose his head, to stop and think. That now everything is really sweet but as the years go by, things get more complicated and when you get to a certain point it can be difficult to get back on course. She intends to tell her own children the same, when the time comes.

We could set the end of our conversation against a background of hand-clapping and guitars. Inma's childhood was much more difficult than her youth. As a child, she says, there are many things you don't understand; you miss your family, you are alone and you feel terrible. When you are a bit older, thanks to the experiences you have lived through, you are more aware of everything, you are a bit tougher and things don't hurt you so much.

Imma's past is the people of Aldeas Infantiles SOS and when, at some time in the future, she leaves, she knows that she will always have something of them in her. She will not be perfect, either in her academic achievements or in the work she does, but I am sure she will be, that she already is, a brilliant person, for the duende she has within her, for the person they have taught her to be. 'This is art!' some will say...

RUBÍ, AN ENTERPRISING SPIRIT

Every corner of Granada, the cultural capital of Andalusia, is steeped in art. In its narrow streets with their white-washed walls spattered with thousands of geraniums, this Andalusian genius can be perceived, this small but vibrant duende of energy and life. This historic city has given Spain, indeed the world as a whole, many great figures from politicians to writers, from musicians to dancers. Of all of them, two in particular come to mind, two women both with a strong personality and temperament, who left their mark on the society of their time: Eugenia de Montijo, Empress of the French, and María La Canastera, one of the best bailaoras of flamenco of recent times. No doubt the Andalusian spirit, strong yet graceful at the same time, marked the personalities of both, converting them into two of the most famous female figures of their time.

However, leaving history to one side, it is not necessary to be an Empress or a great bailaora to stand out in some way or other. This is demonstrated by our young lady from Granada, M. C. P., who we shall call Rubí – ruby for the colour of her hair and ruby for the hardness and, at the same time, the beauty of her character.

I meet Rubí in Madrid, in an Aldeas Infantiles SOS house. She has just arrived from Granada, by bus, together with Mamen and Inma, friends and companions from Aldeas, who I also had the pleasure of talking to and having a good time with. Rubí is the last to arrive in the room where we are to talk. I remember, as she approached to kiss me on both cheeks, an intense perfume, very refreshing on that hot summer afternoon. As she greets me I notice that behind her glasses are hidden eyes that are curious, expectant. I am under observation and the three young women are wondering what I am doing there, so I swiftly answer their questions. Rubí, of all of them, is the one who looks most serene. Something to do with her being the oldest, I suppose.

Introduction – striving to get the better of life

Rubí was born twenty-three years ago in Granada, where she lived with her two younger brothers in a family with severe financial problems. To this material aspect should be added the mental problems of the mother and the difficulties her partner had in dealing with her. These were the causes that led the three children, always together – fortunately, as Rubí notes – to several different children's residential centres such as the Centro Bermúdez de Castro and the Centro Ángel Ganivet. Finally, life, inscrutable at times, brought them to Aldeas Infantiles SOS.

Rubí was taken in by this organisation when she was thirteen, a difficult age, it must be said. There she lived with her two brothers. Two years ago, one of them left to live with his father. The other, the youngest, is still living in one of the Aldeas houses. Today, despite being independent and living in her own flat, Rubí still maintains close contact with the members of her biological family and with what she considers her second family: the people of Aldeas Infantiles SOS. The ten years she spent in this particular family have seen Rubí turn into a woman, mature and responsible despite her tender years, and for what they did for her she feels profoundly grateful.

Rubí has always been a very good student, she tells me, and her friends alongside her nod in agreement. She always got good marks throughout her primary and secondary schooling. Apart from her tenacity and her drive, she recognises that the people at Aldeas have always helped her and encouraged her to carry on with her studies. Anything she has needed – books, private teachers, school material... – she has asked her educators for and they have provided her with it.

Once she had finished her Bachillerato and COU, Rubí had no hesitation in choosing to go on to university as her next objective. Ever since she was very small, she had always wanted to study for a professional career and now the moment had arrived. So, she decided to register for a degree in Business Administration and Management in the Faculty of Economics and Business Studies in the University of Granada. She had always been attracted to these subjects, particularly after doing economics as part of her Bachillerato and finding that she really liked it.

Today, two years after beginning her course, Rubí is studying a Formación Profesional module in Administration and Finance. It is not that she has abandoned her university studies; no, nothing like that, Rubí doesn't give up easily, let me make that very clear. What happened is that she found some of the subjects in the faculty very difficult. The level the university required was too much for her, to the extent that for a time she lost her enthusiasm and the strength to keep going. She doesn't know what happened to her during the first two years in the faculty but, as she says laughingly, she was getting it from all sides. A moment arrived when she couldn't cope any more, she needed to take a break and recover her breath.

Well-advised by the Aldeas psychologist and fearing the onset of a depression, Rubí decided to set aside her university studies and do something different for a while, to breathe some fresh air. A change, she thought, would do her some good. Taking the FP module in Business Administration has turned out to be a very good choice, she says, smiling broadly. The subjects she is doing have allowed her to increase her basic knowledge and I'm sure she will shortly be able to start back at the university. Not being able to finish her degree would be a real thorn in her side. Speaking with Rubí about this you soon realise that graduating has become almost an obsession for her, and given how stubborn she is, as she herself admits, she will manage it soon. Always forward, never backwards, she never tires of repeating to herself.

In the future, if all goes to plan, she will have access to all the opportunities she didn't have when she was younger. She is completely convinced of this, and what is even more important, she says it with no resentment whatsoever. Sooner or later, and no matter how much it takes, I am sure that Rubí will gain her degree – for this is the only thing she is lacking, the official qualification. Even before she has graduated, I can affirm that Rubí is already a businesswoman, and a great risk-taker in all aspects of life, not only professionally but also personally.

By profession, businesswoman

For some time now Rubí, together with her boyfriend, who is also studying Business Administration and Management, has been running her own business, a gift shop in a shopping centre in Granada. There Rubí sells a little of everything – from jewellery to bags, including pendants, bracelets and all kinds of small gifts. I don't know if it is that Rubí doesn't go out of her way to publicise this business, but when I look at her and the way she dresses, the dominant note is one of discretion, with an almost complete absence of the kind of things she sells…

Leaving such observations aside, the truth is that setting up this small business, she explains with a serious gaze, was hard, and it took time to get the capital together. Finally, thanks to her savings, the help of her boyfriend's parents, and a guarantee from Aldeas Infantiles SOS, the couple were able to see their dream come true.

Rubí, nowadays, combines her studies with her shop. With her partner, she shares the work in the business. They take turns – one in the morning, the other in the afternoon. In this way they keep their small business afloat, though recently, and for reasons beyond their control, things are not going as well as they might. As in all businesses, there are good times and bad times. Very often, what they earn does not make up for the hours they have put in, and Rubí knows that sooner or later they will have to close. The profits are often not what they hoped for, and sometimes they don't even cover the costs. However, both she and her boyfriend are optimistic and they don't let it get them down. They have tried and to a large extent they have succeeded in what they set out to do. I am convinced that life will offer them many more opportunities.

The important thing, as Rubí says, is that they have each other, in the flat they share, independent, living their own lives. In fact, setting up the business was the springboard that led them to live together; no doubt one of the best investments in the future they have ever made, and all this at the age of only twenty-one – not very common… Both of them enjoy living as a couple. They help each other and share the housework, and extremely happily, she says laughing. Besides, Rubí has been lucky. She explains, almost gloatingly, that her boyfriend cooks very well and even irons better than her. Often she doesn't have to worry about making a meal – she finds it already done when she arrives home.

Rubí, who is very down-to-earth and many times puts reality first before her hopes and dreams, admits that it's very hard being your own boss and something that she is not yet very good at. Managing her own business, she has learnt a lot in both professional and personal terms, for example, about responsibility and the headaches this involves, besides living with the fact of not knowing how much money she'll have at the end of the month. For all these reasons, she would now like to find another job, one that would offer her a little emotional tranquillity – for there have been times when she has been very anxious – and financial stability, a job where she could do her eight hours and then, once at home, forget all about it until the next day.

It would not be the first time Rubí has had a job like this, for, despite the help from Aldeas Infantiles SOS, she has worked on more than one occasion. She admits she wasn't very happy when they told her she had to find a job, but what could she do? Her first job was in a dried fruit plant. Then she found another job with a large supermarket, stacking shelves and filling in for staff absences – a job she doesn't have very fond memories of. Rubí has often combined work with her studies. It's difficult for her but she gets by. She knows she has less time for studying, but this gives her more strength to keep going. Faced with the pressure of exams, she doesn't let things get on top of her, just the opposite, she knows how to organise herself perfectly well and has no difficulty in concentrating on what she has in hand and, as she says, she studies much better in this way. I think I'd like to ask her how she does this...

A business called life

But where, for the moment, Rubí shows the greatest talent as a risk-taker is in life itself. Luckily, as she herself admits, she has always been able to count on the support of Aldeas Infantiles SOS, especially the educators, who have given her the affection and understanding she needed.

Both she and her two brothers lived with their parents until, for financial and health reasons, they could no longer look after them. For the three children it was a very hard time, but at least they were not separated. They stayed together, as a family. From the time the left the family home, Rubí, much more than an elder sister, became the mother of her two brothers and she has continued to look after them as if they were her own children. In fact, many other children who have lived with her in Aldeas Infantiles SOS over these more than ten years also treat her as their elder sister.

For a girl who is going through adolescence, in fact for any child whatsoever, I think, leaving the home you have been born and brought up in must be one of those difficult times you never forget. But Rubí, conscious at all times of what was best for her and her two brothers, faced up to the situation. From her home in Aldeas, and showing a great sense of responsibility, Rubí looked after her family's money to make sure it wasn't ill-spent. At the same time she took charge of the medical treatment for her mother's mental illness and liver problems. She took her to the doctor, made sure she took her medication and that the social worker was kept informed, amongst other tiresome tasks. This she did, with no complaints, until the end came and her mother finally died. It was an enormous blow for Rubí but the people at Aldeas were at her side, supporting her and making sure she was never alone. She will always be infinitely grateful to them.

But in case it seems otherwise, let me stress that Rubí does not dwell on the sad moments of her life. She describes them with sincerity, without embarrassment, clearly, but does not wallow in them. We all have problems and we are all capable of overcoming them, she says modestly. What happened to her has happened to many other people, and she is sure that some people have had it much worse. Anybody who listens to her, however, cannot fail to feel admiration for the bravery and courage with which she faces life.

In fact, despite the adversities she has been through, Rubí has very fond memories of her time in Aldeas. She considers it the best place she has been in, the only home she has known that she could enjoy without worries. The relationships she has built up with both the educators and with the rest of the children have left their mark on her life. She gets on with them all fantastically well, and if you spend just a few minutes with her, it's easy to understand why.

Her educator Valeria, who she considers to be a mother with a capital 'M', is for Rubí a person she knows she will always be able to count on, someone who will always be at her side whenever she needs her, whenever she has a problem. Having grown up and shared everything with her is something she will never forget. After so many years, she declares with conviction, such a strong bond is created that it would be very difficult to break it. In fact, even though she has her own flat, Rubí still goes to eat at her Aldeas house. Apart from the fact that it is near her work and in this way she can see her younger brother, who is still living there, there is nobody who cooks as well as her SOS mother!

When she looks back, Rubí is surprised by how quickly time has passed. Today, despite the difficulties associated with her university course, Rubí is very proud of having made something of her life, of having done things in the way she believed best, of having invested well and obtained good results, in business terms. But the best thing of all is that she has managed to help her family to keep going, thanks to her sheer willpower and the good advice she has received from the people she has met at Aldeas.

Rubí has learnt much in her short life, whether alone or with the help of others. The most important thing is that everything she has learnt, sometimes the hard way, the values and principles, she would like to pass on to her children, even though at the moment she cannot imagine herself being married. The past, far away in time but very real inside her, is a point of reference she will never forget. However, thinking about this makes her sad. She prefers, instead, to think about the present and the future. Nevertheless, one of the things she will never forget is her time in Aldeas Infantiles SOS and the people she has met there, who she is very grateful to for all they have given her.

When Rubí meets new people, at first she doesn't tell them much about her origins – neither where she is from, nor where she grew up. Later, if the friendship becomes stronger, she has no hesitation about telling them that she is from Aldeas, that her home is Aldeas, that her family is Aldeas. So far, and woe betide anyone who dares to do so, nobody has rejected her as a result. Before, when she was small, she didn't like the fact that when they went camping or on excursions people would point at them and say "Look! Those are the kids from Aldeas!" Now that time has passed. Now talking about Aldeas fills her with pride and happiness.

We leave the room and go out into the garden. On the way, Mauricio, our photographer, takes some pictures of the three young women from Granada. Meanwhile, I carry on asking them questions, out of curiosity, and so that they relax in front of the camera.

When Rubí was small, she liked to daydream and gaze at the stars and the planets. For that reason, she recalls happily, her parents gave her a small telescope that allowed her, with a large dose of imagination, to do so. Rubí wanted to be an astronaut, to fly in a spacecraft and visit the moon. The other two girls laugh, not to make fun of her but out of surprise. Rubí seems so serious, so formal, that they would never have imagined her having such extravagant ideas. For my part, I think that perhaps this dream was a way of escaping the problems she faced on Earth.

This dream, though, is a thing of the past now, and at the moment, Rubí has her feet firmly on the ground. I leave her, in my imagination, doing Tai Chi, an art she says helps her to relax and keep fit. In the distance we hear boleros – one of her favourite types of music. Luis Miguel or Marc Anthony, her favourite singers, sweeten the dreams of this young woman from Granada, whose story, though not that of La Montijo or La Canastera, is one of striving to better herself and which will eventually lead her, no doubt, to cope with one of today's most difficult challenges – being happy.

JONATHAN, AT AN ISLAND RHYTHM

Being born on an island, living there, growing up there is, no doubt, something that marks you. Almost all the island peoples of the world are calm by nature. You only have to visit an island, whatever sea it might be in, to see this for yourself. Their way of speaking, acting or being gives an islander away immediately, whether they like it or not. Looking at this from a positive perspective, it's an enviable way to be. Setting aside, or putting off until tomorrow, the stress and haste of everyday life on the mainland is truly admirable. There's no rush, relax...

Maybe I'm making a generalisation. Of course I am. But in part, I'm not far wrong. With Jonathan you can have no doubts about his island origins, particularly when you hear his accent, that sweet melodic accent of the Canary Islands. But the evidence is conclusive when you see the calmness with which he listens to you, with which he speaks, with which he thinks...

I am introduced to Jonathan in the offices of Aldeas Infantiles SOS in Catalonia, in carrer Ausiàs March in Barcelona. He arrived the day before from Tenerife so that I could interview him. While he is here, he'll use the time to explore the city a little, to explore its streets and alleys and admire its famous sights. Quite a long time has gone by since he first did so.

I find myself faced by a shy, reserved young man, even a little introverted I would say. To all this is added the inevitable nervousness created by the situation. He doesn't know exactly what I am trying to do. I explain it to him, but I don't think he is really convinced.

Let's begin at the beginning. Jonathan González Borges was born twenty-three years ago in Puerto de la Cruz, on the island of Tenerife, in a family that had five children. Shortly after he was born, his parents separated. His mother later rebuilt her life alongside another man, who Jonathan refers to as his step-father. Though his mother's family has always weighed more heavily in his affections, Jonathan continues to see his biological father, who now lives in Santa Úrsula.

Being born into a family with few financial resources, 'poor' is the adjective he uses, resulted in his having a complicated childhood both financially and emotionally. His parents could only provide the basics for survival: food, essential clothing, and not much more.

Jonathan's family, at that time, received some help from third parties that enabled them to keep going and for all the children to go to school. Of this period, Jonathan remembers that once at home, school having finished, he had to help his parents as much as he could: going to the chemist's, doing the shopping, making appointments to see the doctor... If he had time left over, he would go out for a walk and play with any friends he met. Rather than sad, when he talks about this time of his life his words sound empty, blank... Though his parents would have preferred him to help out by bringing some extra money into the house, they didn't try to stop him when, a little older by now, he decided that what he wanted to do was continue studying. Jonathan makes it clear to me that he has always been able to take his decisions with a great deal of freedom.

The financial problems were also the reason why Jonathan had to leave the home he was born in and where he had spent his whole childhood. That situation, as he describes it, evidently did not offer the most propitious, or even adequate, of circumstances in which to grow up. And so, at the age of sixteen, he was admitted to the Sagrada Family, a children's home popularly called La Cuna, in Santa Cruz de Tenerife. There, together with his younger brothers and sisters, he spent just six months. He explains that this change was very hard because he had to leave his whole world behind. Jonathan does not tell me much about life in La Cuna, only that it very different from what he was to find later in Aldeas Infantiles SOS.

It was at this time that the director of Aldeas interviewed him, explained what the centre was and asked him if he was interested in being admitted. In Aldeas Infantiles SOS, he was told, he would not lack anything when it came to studying quietly and being able to live, and that he would have all the support he needed to be able to keep going. In addition, unlike other centres, in Aldeas coming of age was no obstacle. When he reached the age of eighteen, it wasn't a question of being told to stand on his own two feet. Instead, he would be given the chance to stay with them until he was able to support himself by finding a job.

Jonathan talked about it with his younger brothers and sisters, who liked the idea, and they agreed to the move. In the Aldea El Tablero, in Santa Cruz de Tenerife, they spent almost two years, sharing the same house. It was difficult for his two younger brothers to adapt and understand the new situation, but he, being older, coped much better. He confesses that though he has never regretted his decision, he never thought he would be there so long.

During the time he spent in El Tablero, he tells me that his relationship with the educators who were responsible for him was good, though sometimes, as is only to be expected, they had what we might call certain 'differences of opinion'... Just as good was his relationship with the rest of the young people he was living with, most of whom, he tells me, have taken different paths from the one he has chosen. Some have gone out to work, others have left for mainland Spain, or even further afield...

Almost two years after the three brothers were admitted to Aldeas, the situation of their parents improved and the Child Protection Authorities allowed the youngest ones to return to live with them. Jonathan, however, decided to stay where he was. He had almost come of age and asked about the possibility of staying with Aldeas, since he saw it would be the best for him if he wanted to continue studying.

So it was that, on turning eighteen, Jonathan moved into the Youth House Aldeas has for young adults in La Laguna. There, sharing a flat with five other young men from Aldeas Infantiles SOS who, like him, were studying, he was to remain until he was twenty-one. He recognises that at this moment his life took a turn for the better because this change meant greater personal independence for him. He tells me that things went very well there, and he never had any problems with his flatmates, though he admits they could have organised the housework a bit better.

Later, after this very positive experience, Jonathan decided to take a further step and look for a rented flat to share with just two others, one of them also being from Aldeas. The fact that he had to organise his own life, the absolute freedom to go out when he wanted and come in when he wanted, to do his own thing, was, and continues to be, enormously gratifying for him. He has been living there for almost four years now. Aldeas Infantiles SOS continues to support him financially so he can pay for the flat and the associated expenses. He, through his summer jobs, also does what he can to meet these costs.

Jonathan tells me that he is good at housework, in part thanks to the 'mother' he had in the Aldeas house who showed them how to run a home. His free time is occupied with his hobbies: reading and listening to music. When he goes out, alone or with his friends, he likes going to the cinema or to the beach, a pleasure that the people of the Canaries can enjoy almost every day of the year. Jonathan tells me he prefers to go out during the day, though from time to time he also samples the night life.

The importance of education

We leave the offices of Aldeas and set out to wander through the old part of Barcelona. I decide to act as his tourist guide and show him some of the most picturesque corners of the Ribera neighbourhood. Once we are in the Ciutadella park, we head for the Shade House. There, much more relaxed, Jonathan starts to talk about his life as a student.

During his childhood, Jonathan changed schools several times. The experience he had in them was not too good. He, like all children, found some subjects easy and others that he found very difficult. He considers that, in general, it was quite difficult for him to pass the school exams, especially from the age of fourteen onwards, that is, his last year of primary education, and throughout his secondary education. The problem was mainly the financial difficulties his parents were grappling with and which meant that Jonathan had to ask for help to pay for his books and other school expenses.

Another of the difficulties he faced during this period was the relationship he had with some of his classmates. While he had some very good friends at school who he enjoyed himself with, there were others who were very cruel and who picked on him for no apparent reason. He defended himself as best he could, but he was very unhappy. Sometimes he worried about what he would have to deal with the next day, but even though he was afraid, he never let it make him miss a single day of school.

Luckily this situation changed as the years went by. As we get older and the school years pass, he reflects, we come to understand that we can't go on behaving in the same way all our lives, and that we have to live with others and respect them more. As time went by, he and his classmates ended up getting along well together till eventually things were fine almost all the time, though the odd arguments still blew up, almost inevitable, he thinks.

After EGB Jonathan continued to study doing third year of ESO. Even though it was difficult, he wanted to continue learning every day. From then on – or perhaps it was the year after, he's not exactly sure – he began to feel more motivated, wanted to get good marks and to pass the exams. He made up for his lack of basic knowledge of some subjects, like maths and English, which he should have gained in EGB, by doing a special curricular adaptation course, which he voluntarily signed up for when he started ESO. Once he had caught up, he decided to go all out.

When he finished his secondary education, Jonathan asked himself what he really wanted to study – the decision was not at all easy. After looking at the different vocational training options, he chose to do a Mid-Level Formación Profesional course in Administration and Clerical work, with the financial support of Aldeas Infantiles SOS and grants awarded by the Ministry of Education. Once he had completed this course, he decided to try for a higher qualification in the same field. He had seen by this time that this was what he wanted to do. He spent a year preparing for the entrance exam but did not manage to pass it. It was then that he had to decide whether to try to do his Bachillerato or else abandon the idea of studying. The first option won. He completed his two years of Bachillerato with very good academic results and even passed the University Entrance Exam, the PAU.

In June 2006 Jonathan completed the two years of his Higher Level Administration course. He did the two months of practical experience in the University Hospital in La Laguna, something he enjoyed very much. There he spent time in three different departments, had a very good timetable, learnt loads and met many new people. At present he is looking for a job and he says he would love to go back to working in the hospital.

The young people who are over eighteen and who are studying while still in Aldeas Infantiles SOS know what it means to have their keep found and that they must take advantage of any possibility that comes their way to gain professional experience. Jonathan, in the last three years, has devoted his holidays to working, to earn a little money and to improve his CV. He has worked, for example, as an administration assistant in a hotel in Puerto de la Cruz. He has also worked in a kitchen, on the cash-desk of a restaurant and he has done a placement in a financial consultancy, the latter without being paid, as is unfortunately typical here. Today Jonathan feels very satisfied both with his academic and his professional experiences, and feels absolutely ready to step into the world of work.

One of Jonathan's dreams, he tells me, besides being happy, is to get a good job, something that he knows is very important for other aspects of life. He also knows that qualifications and certificates mean little or nothing when it comes to getting a job; the important thing is being able to do the work and knowing how to demonstrate it. He thinks that he could be a good professional. Who knows? Perhaps, with time, he might end up running a company, be the Head of Administration or the Personnel Department, become an accountant, do auditing tasks... His imagination starts to run away with him. Jonathan believes he could do these things, and believing in yourself is, I think, crucial. Later Jonathan comes back down to earth and accepts that if he has to work in a job he doesn't like, or that has nothing to do with what he studied, he will do it. But one thing is clear – if he can, he will always stay in Tenerife... Though he has seen other parts of the country, he is an islander born and bred...

A life of striving to better himself

Little by little, step by step, Jonathan has so far managed to achieve the goals he has set himself, overcoming all the difficulties that he has faced throughout his life in both the personal and academic spheres. He tells me that his way of doing things is to set himself small challenges, short-term goals, things that he attempts to achieve as he goes along, not rushing but not stopping either. Since he realised that what he wanted to do was study, for example, he has set himself a series of objectives and not stopped until he gained the qualifications he wanted. He tells me, not with out a little pride, even though he attempts to hide it, that he has surprised many people who thought he would not get very far in the academic world.

As if defending himself, Jonathan tries to make clear that he has got where he is thanks to his hard work. Nobody has ever given him anything for free, nobody has made things easy for him. He recognises that the people at Aldeas Infantiles SOS, who he will always be very grateful to, have always been there to help him, to support him, to give him a helping hand, but in the end it is he who, through hard work and strength of will, has made a go of his life. Despite everything he has achieved, he is not resting on his laurels and knows that he has to keep on working at everything. Today he feels he has the strength to face the future with greater security in his educational abilities and especially, with greater personal and emotional security.

Jonathan's dependence on Aldeas Infantiles SOS is about to come to an end; in fact it does, just a few months after our meeting, when he finds a job. He tells me he is a little afraid of leaving Aldeas and his student life, and he is not ashamed to say so. It's like leaving behind a life in which he has really been very happy, but he knows that sooner or later the time will come for him to be independent, to stand on his own two feet.

This change of life, not necessarily a radical one, Jonathan sees as something positive – the same way he looks at almost everything. It helps that he is at present enjoying a period of great emotional stability, something that has come with the passing of time, and growing self-confidence. Though he has his bad times, like everybody, and knows that things don't always work out as he would wish, he says he has learnt to trust more in himself and his capacity. He has learnt from his mistakes and from the bad times. This maturity of spirit comes from the fears and anxieties he has had to overcome and that have made him grow as a person.

Though the idea of having children still seems a long way off, Jonathan is sure that he will try to instil in them many of the values he has learnt at Aldeas Infantiles SOS. He wants to teach his children to face life bravely. He will be there for them whenever they need him, protecting them, teaching them… but they will be on their own when it comes to facing the challenges life throws at them. Until the arrival of these children, Jonathan is practising on his younger brothers – he is thirteen years older than the youngest one. He looks out for them, he asks them how things are going, he points out the way they should go and especially, he recommends that they be clear about what they want to do.

Overall, and so far, Jonathan considers that his journey through life has been a great success. Though he has no idea what his future will be, he is clear about one thing, he will continue to be himself – a calm person, one who keeps his word, who is serious and hard-working, and who is respectful towards those above him. Though he tells me he thinks he has always been a good person, much of what he is like now he owes to the people at Aldeas Infantiles SOS, who have knocked off the rough edges. Before, he was more introverted, while in the last few years he has learnt to express his feelings, though he still finds it a bit difficult to do so. He tells me he is still quite reserved because he would feel bad if he bored other people with his problems. I thank him for making an exception with me.

SONIA, WINNING THE MATCH OF HER LIFE

To play tennis, like any other sport, you need to train before you can master the technique, before you learn the tricks of the game, or even its rules, to perfection. Hundreds of hours of training and a careful warm-up are the keys to winning a match. Like tennis, anything we decide to do in life also requires preparation, essential if we want everything to come out as well as possible.

In the case we are going to deal with here, the warm-up sessions must have gone wrong. In fact, something is very wrong when an NGO has to take charge of a newly-born baby. Her biological mother, very young and without the financial resources necessary to look after her child, decided to hand her over to Aldeas Infantiles SOS so that there the baby would receive everything that she, at that moment, and to her very great sadness, was not in a position to give her. Despite this tragic situation, the decision could not have worked out better. Twenty-one years on, we have the chance to see this for ourselves.

There are players who were not born to lose, and who despite all the obstacles they face, know how to come out on top. This is the case of Sonia Loka Builalicopa. I would go so far as to say that

Aldeas has been the only family, in the most literal sense of the word, that she has ever known, though her relationship with her biological mother has never been broken. It has been this family that has given her the means and the necessary tools to keep going, to face up to the adversities, to carve out for herself the present she is currently enjoying and the future that is coming.

Sonia has always been passionate about tennis, a sport she has devoted herself to since she was still a little girl. Despite the many competitions she has played in, with their victories and their defeats, the most important match she has played has been against life itself, a very experienced opponent, and one who seemed to hold all the aces. But sometimes, strength of will is the key when it comes to facing even the best player.

15–0

Sonia began to gain an advantage in this particular match at the moment she entered Aldeas Infantiles SOS in San Lorenzo de El Escorial. The circumstances facing her biological mother meant that she was accepted into the Madrid Aldea. This was to be, until she became an adult, Sonia's home. I ask her what she thought of all these years, her whole life in Aldeas. I thought she might make some comparison with a conventional family life, but Sonia answers that she has known no other life, and so what she has lived in the Aldea seems marvellous to her. Good times and bad times, days of laughter and others of tears… Normal things, just like everybody.

30–0

Childhood and adolescence were happy times in Aldeas for this very responsible girl, sporty and cheerful, who felt protected at all times by the eight other children, her 'brothers and sisters' in the home.

It's true that they are not blood brothers and sisters, but she feels very close to them, and loves them as if they were. When it comes down to it, they are the only ones she has and she has lived with them for many years now. Being in close contact makes you close, but listening to Sonia talking about them, you realise they are much more than close.

Her first memories, though disjointed, of her infancy in Aldeas go back to when she was three or four. From seven onwards, she remembers many more things. When she was very small, Sonia had two different tutors but, naturally, given the age she was when she was admitted, she remembers nothing of them. Very soon, though, Mª José appeared as the person who was to represent for Sonia the mother figure, that person who was always to be at her side, not only to educate her but also to support and encourage her. However, her biological mother has continued seeing her and visiting her from when she was admitted into Aldeas right up until now. Thus, Sonia has been a lucky girl, for many years she has had two mothers.

Her seven brothers and sisters, the children she lived with until she left the Aldeas house, form, together with Mª José, an authentic family. Sonia goes much further and tells me that in age she is the fifth. She celebrates her birthdays with them, her holidays, her Christmases... with them she has shared joy, sadness and experiences of all kinds. They lived all together from the age of three until eleven in one of the houses Aldeas Infantiles SOS has in San Lorenzo de El Escorial. Afterwards, they were moved to another house, but outside this area – they went to live on a nearby estate. This was because they had to make way for the other children who were joining this great family.

In October 2004, at the age of twenty, Sonia left her beloved Mª José and her brothers and sisters and went to live in the supervised accomodation that Aldeas Infantiles SOS has in Monte Escorial. The separation was very hard, she admits, but with time she gradually got over it. At present Sonia shares the flat with two other young women, Nora and Esperanza – the latter another of our interviewees. The follow-up work is done by Maribel, who we know they get on very well with. Now, she explains, there is nobody to put food in front of them, nor do the ironing for them, nor the washing. The three of them have to arrange things so that they can find the time for both their studies and the housework.

From here, if all goes to plan, Sonia will finally become independent and lead a normal life, just like any other young person of her age. When Sonia is completely autonomous, her relationship with Aldeas Infantiles SOS will officially have come to an end, though I am sure she will always keep the people there in her heart. From what she tells me, and from how she tells it, I'd say that her independence is just around the corner.

40–0

At the age of twenty-one, Sonia looks back on her life and comments on the fact that she has never been able to celebrate Fathers' Day or Mothers' Day. Even so, she feels happy and grateful. She knows that she lived a full and happy childhood and never lacked for anything. And it was a childhood in which she was even able to allow herself the luxury of doing what she liked. She has always been able to play a sport, tennis, which seemed to be reserved for the privileged few, though she hastens to correct this idea.

One day, at the age of eight, whilst in primary education at the state school in San Lorenzo de El Escorial, she and her brothers and sisters were offered the chance to do some after-school activity. Faced with the option of sports, drawing or music classes, Sonia chose the first. The older children in her house already played tennis and she didn't want to be left out.

Little by little, Sonia began to develop a passion for the sport. First she trained in a sports centre till it ended up being demolished. Then, seeing that Sonia really liked tennis, she began training in various clubs, competing in teams within the Comunidad de Madrid. Later, and so that she could combine tennis with her schoolwork, she found a club in Villalba where she played for several years.

2 Games to Love

Sonia clocks up points in her life in the same way she does when playing tennis. She stands tall when faced with adversities, and draws strength from them so that she can find their weak points against which to direct all her energy. Knowing the importance of education, both as a young girl and in secondary school, she passed all her exams without any problems. Her secondary schooling was also in the state school in San Lorenzo de El Escorial, though when she decided to do the Arts Bachillerato she had to change school and go to Villalba (Madrid). Sonia has never stopped studying, even though she doesn't enjoy it as much as sport. Though she didn't get excellent marks, she passed each year without problem. She still has many good friends from this period, who she sees as often as she can.

The Arts Bachillerato, for its part, opened the doors to what was to become her other great passion: graphic design. In this sector, in which she is still studying, she has found a way of making a living at the same time as enjoying herself since she is doing something she really likes – and this, I think, is extremely difficult nowadays.

At first, having finished her Bachillerato, Sonia had thought about taking a university degree in Fine Arts, since she had always liked painting and drawing ever since she was very small. However, when she saw how few chances she would have of working in this field, she gave up the idea. It was then that, through the godmother of one of the girls in the home, she tells me all this in great detail, she discovered the world of graphic design. She hadn't known that it was possible to get a qualification in this and, as soon as she found out, she was drawn to the idea. After passing the entrance exam, she began her arts and design course, to her great excitement, with excellent results. Sonia tells me she would like to work in publishing design. I think about the designers I work with, very good professionals, and I believe she's got what it takes.

3 Games to Love

Sonia knows how difficult it sometimes is to achieve your goal, and yet, she believes that it is possible to do so if you dedicate enough energy to it. That's why, while she continues studying every morning, she devotes two afternoons a week to preparing a school magazine with children from the fifth year of primary; at the same time, her weekends are for giving tennis classes. In summer, when the weather and the timetable permit, these classes are intensive. She teaches on the estate where her flat is. Her pupils are between four and sixteen years old, though from time to time she also gives classes to some adults. In this way, Sonia is able to make money from what she likes doing, feel fulfilled and help her to pay her keep and her day-to-day expenses, which for the moment Aldeas Infantiles SOS continues to underwrite.

She stopped participating in competitions, she tells me, because it was very difficult to combine with her education. A very good monitor encouraged her to give classes, an excellent way of not losing contact with tennis, and she took the advice. If some years ago she had been told that she would now be working with young children and, what can sometimes be worse, with their parents, she would not have believed it. Sonia is conscious that it is a job that involves a lot of responsibility and patience, things she can now offer because she has grown up a lot. Some years ago, it would have been impossible for her to do something like this.

4 Games to Love

Two summers ago she had the chance to go to Chicago to see another way of life, part of a student exchange programme. She didn't want to miss out on the opportunity, and, as would have been the case with any young person of her age, this led to what has so far been her best experience, her best memory. Days of leisure, of seeing the sights and of fun, which she was able to enjoy while feeling just like anybody else, a lucky student taking advantage of the chance to see a new culture, to learn a language, to mix with people other than those she is normally surrounded by.

Now she would like to go abroad again, preferably to an English speaking country, and spend a while there. She would like to become proficient in this language because she has seen that it really is necessary in many fields of life, especially in graphic design. When I ask her how she sees herself in five years time, the response is what you would expect: in a good situation professionally speaking, as independent as possible in all senses, and, above all, combining work with playing tennis. Very clear.

5 Games to Love

Sonia considers herself to be very fortunate. She knows that she is still a student, and that this period of her life is one of the best she will ever live. She's trying to get as much as she possibly can out of it, conscious as she is that people who work have very little time for themselves. She wants to continue playing tennis, meeting up with her friends from school, with her brothers and sisters from Aldeas and with her flatmates. Listening to her, it sometimes seems as though she is still a child, still living in that cotton-wool padded world, but her way of explaining things makes it clear that, just when it's least expected, she will take off and fly.

6 Games to Love

Optimistic by nature, Sonia sees that she has been privileged to have the life she has had. "At my age, many people don't even know how to look after themselves", she says confidently. "They live at home, waiting for the food to be put in front of them, for their beds to be made. Meanwhile, I'm lucky enough to live in a flat where I look after myself". And though she knows she will have to conjure up non-existent time from somewhere or another, she enjoys what she does and that makes her feel good.

Game, set and match

It's true that as a girl her dream was to become a famous tennis player, but it's also true that many young girls dream of being princesses, and they never make it. Sonia knows that she has done much more than that. She has established herself in the world like any other person, even though everything was against her at the beginning.

When I ask her about this, she says she firmly believes that her story demonstrates her determination to overcome the difficulties she has faced. Even though she has always had the unconditional support of Aldeas Infantiles SOS, it has been her hard work that has got her to where she is now. Is it possible for any more important dream than this to come true?

DREAMS COME TRUE

The objective of the VITALISE Project is simply that of helping to make come true the dreams of some of the young people from ALDEAS INFANTILES SOS who have decided to keep going with their studies and fulfil their academic goals. Through the SUEÑOS HOSPES scholarships, the young men and women, apart from having their educational and living costs covered, will also have available to them some extra support. ALDEAS INFANTILES SOS, charged with the tutelage of these young people while they are studying, will be responsible for managing the monies paid over as study grants.

The process that the young people followed from the moment these study grants were announced until the verdict of the Jury was made known was relatively simple. After being selected by ALDEAS INFANTILES SOS, and having complied with the essential prerequisites for obtaining the grant, their projects were presented to the Jury either by the Directors of their respective Aldeas or by the Directors of the Social Programme Centres (CPS). The Sueños Jury was made up of representatives of HOSPES, Aldeas Infantiles SOS, the AIPS – the Iberian Association of Sleep Pathology – together with other persons who have stood out for their capacity to fulfil their DREAM during their professional or personal career.

Of all the projects presented, the Jury, after many hours of deliberations, discussions and debate, finally managed to choose the winners of the three grants, each one worth some 6000 euros. The winners were Rubí, David Lago and Jonathan González. And so, the three young people can see that, little by little, their dreams are beginning to take shape.

As for Rubí, from Granada, when she was told, the decision took her by surprise. She could not believe that, of all her companions, she had been selected as a winner of the study grant. The money will enable her to continue studying the module in Administration and Finance that she is currently doing. When she finishes this, her intention is to complete her degree in Business Administration and Management that she began a couple of years ago in the Faculty of Economics and Business Studies at the University of Granada and which, for various reasons, she had to put temporarily to one side. Despite having her own business in a shopping centre in Granada, Rubí is still not in a very stable financial situation, so the money from this grant will help her enormously.

David Lago, from Galicia, did not overreact when he was told that he was one of the Hospes 2005 study grant winners – not because he was not overjoyed but simply because that is his character: calm, relaxed, always in control of the situation… Obviously, and even though he does not show it, he is very proud and satisfied to have obtained the study grant that doubtless will help him to enjoy his final year as a student and complete his graduation project, a necessary prerequisite for obtaining the qualification of Mining Engineer. The truth is that David never imagined that he would be one of the winners of the grant, and so he shows little excitement when he talks about it – as if he still didn't quite believe it.

The other young person from Aldeas Infantiles SOS who received the Hospes 2005 grant was Jonathan González from Tenerife, born and brought up in Puerto de la Cruz. For him, the grant, rather than its material importance, means the recognition of a long and hard struggle that, since he was small, he has had to engage in for his dreams to come true. His goals have long been to study and assure for himself a decent place in life. The money from the grant, apart from covering any incidental expenses he might have, will enable him to complete the second and final year of his Higher Level course in Administration. The happiness he feels about winning the study grant would be complete if he managed to find a job of the kind he aspires to and that, as he puts it, would enable him to work as professionally as possible.

With the awarding of these study grants, then, the efforts of three young people have been rewarded, youngsters who have struggled long and hard to overcome the difficulties they faced and have come out on top. Their academic achievements, their commitment and capacity to give of themselves generously to others and their constancy, their unending hard work, have found their just reward.

ᶜUF̃Ɔᶜ

There is something even greater than making your own dreams come true.
Making the dreams of another person come true.

The *Sueños* Project is a social, non-profit making initiative, designed and developed by Hospes with one single aim: that of highlighting the true sense of the word SUEÑO. How to achieve this? By taking its two etymological senses and, with imagination and strength of will, making each of them become a reality through a particular project:

By helping young people from **Aldeas Infantiles SOS** to achieve their personal and professional dreams, offering three study grants each year.

Aldeas Infantiles SOS de España

By promoting scientific research into sleep patterns in collaboration with **IASP** (Iberian Association of Sleep Pathology), awarding an annual prize to the best international research project investigating sleep patterns.

Welcome to the
culture of *Sueños*.

www.hospes.es/suenos